T0135969

Studien zur Mustererkennung

herausgegeben von:

Prof. Dr.-Ing. Heinrich Niemann
Prof. Dr.-Ing. Elmar Nöth

Bibliografische Information der Deutschen Nationalbibliothek

Die Deutsche Nationalbibliothek verzeichnet diese Publikation in der
Deutschen Nationalbibliografie; detaillierte bibliografische Daten sind
im Internet über http://dnb.d-nb.de abrufbar.

©Copyright Logos Verlag Berlin GmbH 2010
Alle Rechte vorbehalten.

ISBN 978-3-8325-2631-3
ISSN 1617-0695

Logos Verlag Berlin GmbH
Comeniushof
Gubener Str. 47
10243 Berlin
Tel.: +49 030 42 85 10 90
Fax: +49 030 42 85 10 92
INTERNET: http://www.logos-verlag.de

Probabilistic Modeling for Segmentation in Magnetic Resonance Images of the Human Brain

(Wahrscheinlichkeitstheoretische Modellierung für die Segmentierung in Magnetresonanztomographieaufnahmen des menschlichen Gehirns)

Der Technischen Fakultät der
Universität Erlangen-Nürnberg

zur Erlangung des Grades

DOKTOR-INGENIEUR

vorgelegt von

Michael Wels

Erlangen – 2010

Als Dissertation genehmigt von der
Technischen Fakultät der
Universität Erlangen-Nürnberg

Tag der Einreichung: 12.02.2010
Tag der Promotion: 15.06.2010
Dekan: Prof. Dr.-Ing. R. German
Berichterstatter: Prof. Dr.-Ing. J. Hornegger
                         Prof. Dr. G. Székely

To my family, my parents, and my sister.

Acknowledgments

A debt of gratitude to my supervisors Prof. Joachim Hornegger, PhD, Dorin Comaniciu, PhD, and Martin Huber, PhD, and their institutions, i.e., the University of Erlangen-Nuremberg and the Siemens AG, for their willingness to financially support the research activities this piece of work provides record of. Also, for providing excellent working environments with teams naturally contributing cutting edge technologies as part of their daily work. I am proud and feel honored for having had the opportunity to conduct my PhD studies together with their groups at the University of Erlangen-Nuremberg's Pattern Recognition Lab in Erlangen, Germany, at Siemens Corporate Technology's SE 5 SCR 2 department in Erlangen, Germany, and at Siemens Corporate Research's Integrated Data Systems department in Princeton, NJ, USA.

I would like to express my thanks to Prof. Gábor Székely, PhD, from the ETH Zürich's Computer Vision Laboratory for agreeing to review this thesis. I deeply appreciate the honor given to me herewith.

I am very grateful to my direct supervisors Gustavo Carneiro, PhD, and Yefeng Zheng, PhD, for their remarkable expertise in the field of data-base guided medical image segmentation, and their leadership skills making working together with them efficient, effective, and also very rewarding. I enjoyed being part of their teams and being able to ask them for help at any time.

Special thanks to my fellow colleagues in the aforementioned groups for their methodological and technological support, inspiring discussions, their honest feedback and the favorable reception I experienced both in Erlangen as well as in Princeton. In particular I would like to thank Prof. Elmar Nöth, PhD, Prof. Elli Angelopoulou, PhD, Florian Jäger, Yu Deuerling-Zheng, Andreas Wimmer, Ingmar Voigt, Dieter Hahn, PhD, Michael Balda, Anja Borsdorf, PhD, Eva Kollorz, Christian Riess, Christian Schaller, Benjamin Keck, Andreas Maier, PhD, Martin Spiegel, Michael Lynch, PhD, Alexey Tsymbal, PhD, Cristian Mircean, PhD, Sascha Seifert, PhD, Michael Kelm, PhD, María Jimena Costa, PhD, Paul Pandea, Terrence Chen, PhD, Bogdan Georgescu, PhD, Alexander Schwing and Zhuowen Tu, PhD.

Many thanks to Prof. Martin Styner, PhD, Tobias Heimann, PhD, and Prof. Bram van Ginneken, PhD, for giving me the opportunity to take part in the MICCAI 2007 Workshop on 3D Segmentation in the Clinic: A Grand Challenge competition and their efforts in establishing new benchmarking possibilities for medial image segmentation algorithms.

Thanks to Alessandro Rossi, MD, Prof. Gundula Staatz, MD, Alexander Aplas, MD, Clement Vachet, and Paul Pandea for providing data for my research and helping to generate ground-truth annotations.

Thanks also to Elsevier Limited for kindly granting permission to reprint material from Gray's Anatomy [104].

Michael Wels

Abstract

This thesis deals with the fully automatic generation of semantic annotations for medical imaging data by means of medical image segmentation and labeling. In particular, we focus on the segmentation of the human brain and related structures from magnetic resonance imaging (MRI) data. We present three novel probabilistic methods from the field of database-guided knowledge-based medical image segmentation. We apply each of our methods to one of three MRI segmentation scenarios: 1) 3-D MRI brain tissue classification and intensity non-uniformity correction, 2) pediatric brain cancer segmentation in multi-spectral 3-D MRI, and 3) 3-D MRI anatomical brain structure segmentation. All the newly developed methods make use of domain knowledge encoded by probabilistic boosting-trees (PBT), which is a recent machine learning technique. For all the methods we present uniform probabilistic formalisms that group the methods into the broader context of probabilistic modeling for the purpose of image segmentation. We show by comparison with other methods from the literature that in all the scenarios our newly developed algorithms in most cases give more accurate results and have a lower computational cost. Evaluation on publicly available benchmarking data sets ensures reliable comparability of our results to those of other current and future methods. We also document the participation of one of our methods in the ongoing online caudate segmentation challenge (www.cause07.org), where we rank among the top five methods for this particular segmentation scenario.

Kurzfassung

Thema dieser Arbeit ist die vollautomatische Bereitstellung semantischer Annotationen für medizinisches Bildmaterial. Hierzu werden Segmentierungs- und Segmenterkennungstechniken aus der medizinischen Bildverarbeitung verwandt. Ausgangspunkt der Betrachtungen sind Magnetresonanztomographieaufnahmen (MRT-Aufnahmen) des menschlichen Gehirns. Hierfür präsentieren wir drei neuentwickelte datenbankgetriebene, wissensbasierte Segmentierungsverfahren. Alle Verfahren werden jeweils in einem von drei Segmentierungsszenarios aus dem Bereich der neuroradiologischen Magnetresonanztomographie (MRT) angewandt: Wir befassen uns erstens mit der Gewebeklassifikation und Korrektur von Magnetfeldinhomogenitäten in 3-D MRT-Aufnahmen des Gehirns, zweitens mit der Segmentierung pädiatrischer Hirntumore in multi-spektralen 3-D MRT-Aufnahmen und drittens mit der Segmentierung anatomischer Hirnstrukturen in 3-D MRT-Aufnahmen. Die Probabilistic Boosting-Tree-Technik (PBT-Technik) aus dem Bereich des maschinellen Lernens bildet die gemeinsame Kernkomponente der drei neuentwickelten Methoden. Sie alle sind durchgängig wahrscheinlichkeitstheoretisch formuliert und können daher in den Gesamtkontext der probabilistische Modelle nutzenden Bildsegmentierungsverfahren eingruppiert werden. In allen drei Szenarios zeigen Vergleiche zu anderen den neuesten Stand der Technik repräsentierenden Methoden, dass unsere neuentwickelten Algorithmen in den meisten Fällen bei geringerem Rechenaufwand akkuratere Ergebnisse liefern. Durch die Verwendung von frei verfügbaren Benchmark-Datensätzen wird die verlässliche Vergleichbarkeit unserer Evaluationsergebnisse auch hinsichtlich künftiger Verfahren gewährleistet. Darüber hinaus dokumentieren wir in dieser Arbeit die Teilnahme einer unserer Methoden am fortgesetzten "Online Caudate Segmentation Challenge"-Wettbewerb (www.cause07.org), bei dem wir unter den fünf besten Segmentierungsverfahren für das dortige Szenario rangieren.

Contents

List of Figures

List of Tables

Chapter 1

Introduction

1.1 The Human Brain

The brain or encephalon is a component of the human central nervous system (CNS). It lies in the cranial cavity and is enveloped by a system of membranes—the so-called meninges. According to reference [96], it can be divided into six parts:

1. the myelencephalon or medulla oblongata,

2. the pons,

3. the mesencephalon or midbrain,

4. the cerebellum,

5. the diencephalon or interbrain, and

6. the telencephalon, cerebrum, or great brain.

The first three parts form the brainstem, which, for instance, contains cardiac and respiratory centers. [96]

The cerebellum primarily holds important parts of the motor system. [96]

The interbrain contains, among other things, the thalamus and the hypothalamus. The thalamus relays sensation, special sense and motor signals from the peripheral nervous system to the great brain. The hypothalamus contains several control centers of the autonomic nervous system. They regulate a number of vital functions like body temperature and the body's water and energy balance. [3]

The great brain, being the largest part of the human brain, is separated into the two equal sized cerebral hemispheres with respect to the midsagittal plane. The corpus callosum is the only connection between them. The surface of the cerebrum, that is to say, the cerebral cortex, consists of elevations or gyri and depressions or sulci. On a cellular level, the cortex is formed by neurons and their unmyelinated fibers causing the tissue to appear gray during dissection or in anatomical specimens. The hippocampus, for instance, is a cortical part of the limbic system, which is associated with congenital and acquired behavior and the origin of drive, motivation, and emotion. [96] In contrast, the white matter (WM) below the cortical gray matter (GM) of the cortex is composed of myelinated axons interconnecting different regions of the CNS. However, there are sub-cortical GM structures or nuclei embedded in the cerebral WM like the basal ganglia consisting of the putamen, the caudate nucleus, the globi pallidi, the subthalamic nucleus, and the substantia nigra. The basal ganglia are associated with a variety of functions, among other things, motor control [96]. Also parts of the limbic system like the amygdala are sub-cortical nuclei. Figs. 1.1 and 1.2 give an overview of the anatomical structures within the cerebrum. [33, 104]

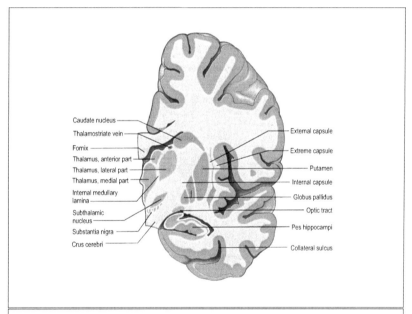

Figure 1.1: Coronal section of the human brain. From Gray's Anatomy [104], p. 311. Reprinted with permission from copyright holder.

Both the brain and the spinal chord are surrounded by cerebral spinal fluid (CSF) or liquor cerebrospinalis. It is produced and circulates in the ventricular system consisting of the right and left lateral ventricles (see Figs. 1.1 and 1.2) and the third and fourth ventricle. The ventricular system is connected to the exterior of the spinal chord and cerebral hemispheres via the apertures and the cerebellomedullary cistern. Occupying the space between the arachnoid mater, that is, the middle layer of the meninges and the pia mater,

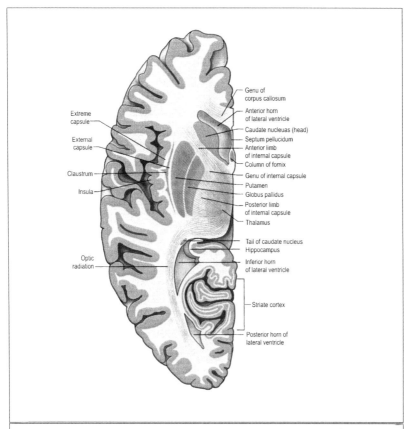

Genu of
corpus callosum

Anterior horn
of lateral ventricle

Caudate nucleus (head)

Septum pellucidum

Anterior limb
of internal capsule

Column of fornix

Genu of internal capsule

Putamen

Globus pallidus

Posterior limb
of internal capsule

Thalamus

Tail of caudate nucleus

Hippocampus

Inferior horn
of lateral ventricle

Striate cortex

Posterior horn of
lateral ventricle

Extreme
capsule

External
capsule

Claustrum

Insula

Optic
radiation

Figure 1.2: Axial section of the human brain. From Gray's Anatomy [104], p. 328. Reprinted with permission from copyright holder.

that is, the innermost layer of the meninges, the CSF mechanically protects the brain but also distributes neuroendocrine factors and prevents brain ischemia. [96]

The brain can be affected by lesions, which can be either intra-axial, i.e., within the brain, or extra-axial, i.e., outside the brain. Meningiomas, which arise from the meninges, and acoustic neuromas are typical extra-axial tumors. Intra-axial lesions can be primary or secondary, in which secondary brain lesions are the most common type. They can be metastatic tumor deposits, for example, from breast or lung carcinoma, or can be caused by metastatic infection. Primary brain lesions are less frequent and range from benign to extremely aggressive with a poor prognosis. Arising from different cell lines they include gliomas, oligodendrocytomas, and choroid plexus tumors. Though occurring at any age there are two peaks of incidence: one in the first few years of life and the other later in the early to middle age. [33]

In the case of a conspicuous anamnesis it is a standard procedure to guide further neurological differential diagnosis by means of radiological imaging. Amongst the various imaging modalities used, magnetic resonance imaging (MRI) usually shows a higher soft tissue contrast than computed tomography (CT) or traditional X-ray imaging, which makes MRI the method of choice especially for neuroradiological examinations. Moreover, MRI, together with ultrasound (US) imaging, does not expose patients to any ionizing radiation during image acquisition and is therefore virtually harmless. Both MRI and US are therefore also well-suited for the radiological examination of pediatric patients.

1.2   Magnetic Resonance Imaging

In the following we give a short introduction to the principles of MRI, which is also known as magnetic resonance tomography (MRT). It follows the representation of Laubenberger and Laubenberger [68] with additional information taken from Weishaupt et al. [117]. A more detailed description can be found in reference [15].

The phenomenon of nuclear magnetic resonance (NMR) was independently discovered by F. Block and G. M. Purcell in 1946. In 1974 P. C. Lauterbur was the first to use MRI to picture a living organism: a mouse. The first magnetic resonance (MR) image of the human body, depicting a thorax, was acquired in 1977 by P. Mansfield.

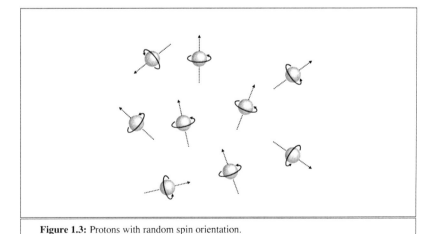

Figure 1.3: Protons with random spin orientation.

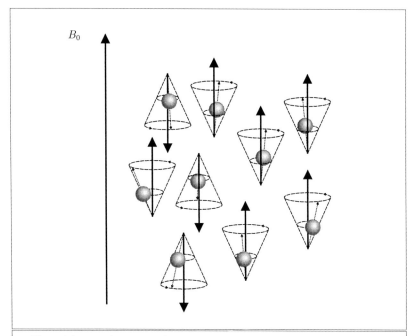

Figure 1.4: Precessing protons after parallel or anti-parallel alignment of spins due to the external magnetic field B_0.

All atomic nuclei with an odd number of protons (atomic number) feature a spin or magnetic moment, that is, the nuclei rotate about their own axes like spinning tops as shown in Fig. 1.3. Hydrogen, nitrate, sodium, and phosphor, for instance, are some of the atoms sharing this property. Among these atoms, hydrogen is the most frequently found atom in living tissues such that, almost exclusively, hydrogen atoms contribute to todays clinical MR image generation.

In an MRI scanner (see Fig. 1.5(a)) the protons' spin axes are aligned, parallel or antiparallel, with the streamlines of the strong external magnetic field (B_0 field) of the scanner building up a stable state longitudinal magnetization along the z-axis (see Fig. 1.5(b)). Additionally, due to the external field, the axes start precessing about the axis of alignment (z-axis) similar to a spinning top. The characteristic speed of this precession is called Larmor or precession frequency ω_0 [MHz], which is proportional to the strength B_0 [T] of the external magnetic field, that is,

$$\omega_0 = \gamma_0 \cdot B_0 \tag{1.1}$$

where γ_0 is the gyromagnetic ratio of the type of nuclei of interest. Both phenomena, parallel or antiparallel alignment and precession, are depicted in Fig. 1.4. The orientation of the spins as well as their phase coherence can be altered by radio frequency (RF) pulses having the same frequency as the Larmor frequency. A $90°$ pulse, for instance, causes the spins rotating about the z-axis to also rotate about the axis induced by the RF pulse, which, due to having exactly the same frequency, appears to be static from the spins' relative point of view. The resulting complex movement of spins statistically cancels longitudinal magnetization along the z-axis and establishes transversal magnetization rotating in phase within the xy-plane (see Fig. 1.5(b)). The latter can be measured with the MRI scanner's receiver coils. Immediately after excitation with an RF pulse, the equilibrium state longitudinal magnetization starts to recover causing transverse magnetization to fade. This process is called T1, longitudinal, or spin-lattice relaxation. Also phase coherence gradually vanishes thereby additionally decreasing transverse magnetization. The process of dephasing is called T2, transverse, or spin-spin relaxation.

The duration of both kinds of relaxation is constant for specific substances. Different pulse sequences make use of this fact and regulate the scanner's sensitivity to certain relaxation parameters (T1-weighted or T2-weighted imaging). According to the weighting, certain substances or organs appear brighter or darker in the acquired image dependant on their proton density.

In order to spatially resolve the location of the received MR signal, that is, the measured change of transverse magnetization over time, additional gradient coils covering the three dimensions of real space are used. They vary locally the external magnetic field B_0. Thus, in accordance with Equation (1.1) excitation can be steered to specific locations by the strength of the RF pulses applied. This makes MRI an inherent 3-D radiological imaging modality where no tomographic reconstruction from several planar, that is, 2-D, projections is required as it is the case, for instance, in CT imaging.

However, the 3-D images acquired need interpretation by a trained expert radiologist. He or she knows which part of the body and which organs in particular are to be seen on the images. With the help of his anatomical knowledge his perception is enriched by a certain understanding of the decomposition of the depicted scene into meaningful, not merely anatomical, entities. A subtle analysis of the image at hand immediately takes place without being necessarily apperceived as a mental event on its own behalf by the observer himself. This differs entirely from how a computer "perceives" not only radiological but images, in the common sense, in general; namely recognizing them as what they in fact are by definition—nothing but a volume or matrix of signal measurements. Bridging the gap between mere data and a preferably automatically generated semantic description of the depicted content is an important aspect within the scientific field of medical image analysis. This general problem can be decomposed into several steps ranging from relatively concrete to very abstract interpretations of the image content. In the early stages it

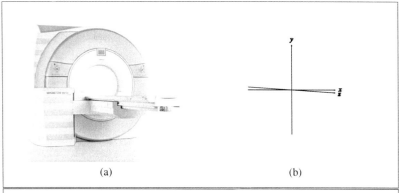

Figure 1.5: The modern MRI scanner Siemens MAGNETOM Verio 3T (www.medical.siemens.com, 07/24/2009) (a) and its associated coordinate system (b).

is mostly useful to address image segmentation and labeling, that is, uniquely identifying certain image regions as meaningful entities.

1.3 Medical Image Segmentation

In the following we give a formal description of the problem of medical image segmentation and labeling, which is the problem of giving semantic information to coherent image regions. These preliminary remarks are necessary as in the course of this thesis three medical image segmentation scenarios will be discussed in order to exemplify the potential of our newly developed machine learning-based and database-guided algorithms for segmenting and labeling 3-D brain MR images.

Let the family $X = (x_s)_{s \in S}$ be a 2-D, that is, $S = \{1, \ldots, X\} \times \{1, \ldots, Y\}$, or 3-D, that is, $S = \{1, \ldots, X\} \times \{1, \ldots, Y\} \times \{1, \ldots, Z\}$, $X, Y, Z \in \mathbb{N}^+$, medical image. Its values or measurements $x_s \in \mathbb{R}^n$, $n \in \mathbb{N}^+$, can be either scalar, $n = 1$, or multi-spectral, $n > 1$. The latter is sometimes also called a vector-valued or multi-channel medical image [84]. The x_s are usually quantified in an appropriate manner for electronic processing. As it will be $S = \{1, \ldots, X\} \times \{1, \ldots, Y\} \times \{1, \ldots, Z\}$ in most parts of this thesis we will refer to the s as image voxels.

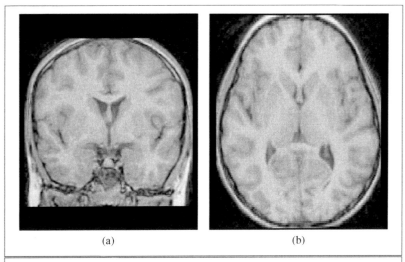

(a)   (b)

Figure 1.6: Coronal (a) and axial (b) section of the human brain in a typical T1-weighted 3-D MRI scan. From the Internet Brain Segmentation Repository (IBSR), www.cma.mgh.harvard.edu/ibsr.

Following Pham et al. [84], the problem of image segmentation (without labeling) can be defined as the search for a partition of an image, i.e., a partition of the set of its voxels, into homogeneous and connected regions. Formally, one searches for

$$S = \bigcup_{k=1}^{K} S_k \tag{1.2}$$

where

$$\forall_{i,j \in \{1,\dots,K\}, i \neq j} \, S_i \cap S_j = \emptyset \tag{1.3}$$

and

$$\forall_{x_s, x_t \in S_k, k \in \{1,\dots,K\}} \, \exists_{(s_l)_{1,\dots,L}, L \in \mathbb{N}^+, s_1 = s, s_L = t} \, \forall_{i \in \{1,\dots,L\}} \, |s_{i-1} - s_i| \leq 1 \tag{1.4}$$

or

$$\forall_{x_s, x_t \in S_k, k \in \{1,\dots,K\}} \, \exists_{(s_l)_{1,\dots,L}, L \in \mathbb{N}^+, s_1 = s, s_L = t} \, \forall_{i \in \{1,\dots,L\}} \, \max_{d \in \{1,2,3\}} |s_{(i-1)_d} - s_{i_d}| \leq 1 \tag{1.5}$$

depending on whether a 3-D 6-neighborhood or 26-neighborhood is considered, respectively.

Ideally, every S_k corresponds to an anatomical structure or other, from a physician's view, meaningful entity in the image. The requirement of connectedness is sometimes relaxed such that actually a classification problem instead of a classical segmentation problem is addressed. This is occasionally of interest in medical imaging when multiple regions of the same tissue class are about to be detected. The total number of tissue classes, K, is usually determined based on prior knowledge about the anatomy considered. In the case of brain MR images, for instance, it is common practice to assume $K = 3$ tissue classes: GM, WM, and CSF. [84]

The process of assigning a descriptive designation to each of the resulting segments is called labeling. Though formally independent from each other we will never address pure image segmentation without labeling throughout this thesis. So, whenever we talk of image segmentation we actually mean image segmentation and region labeling.

1.4 Knowledge-Based Approaches to Medical Image Segmentation

Throughout this thesis, we focus on the application of knowledge-based approaches to medical image segmentation integrating domain knowledge across several layers of geometrical abstraction. In particular, we follow the paradigm of database-guided medical image segmentation [44] where the vast majority of domain knowledge used to guide the segmentation process is initially represented by large collections of medical imaging data with accompanying ground-truth segmentations. Models are generated from these databases by means of machine learning techniques. These models are then used, often in combination with traditional techniques, for image segmentation.

We explore the capabilities of three newly developed segmentation algorithms of that kind in three distinct scenarios from the broader field of 3-D brain MR image segmentation: 3-D MRI brain tissue classification and intensity non-uniformity (INU) correction, pediatric brain tumor segmentation in 3-D MRI, and 3-D MRI brain structure segmentation. We are able to show by experimental validation that our knowledge-based approaches outperform most of the current state-of-the-art methods to these particular segmentation challenges with respect to segmentation accuracy (see Chapters 2–4) and also with respect to computation time (see Chapters 3 and 4). The results obtained and the current state-of-the-art to be found in the literature (see Chapters 2–4) encourage us to advance the hypothesis that database-guided knowledge-based approaches state the answer both to today's as well as to tomorrow's medical image segmentation challenges.

1.5 EU Research Project Health-e-Child

The research efforts on providing semantic descriptions of MR images of the human brain by means of medical image segmentation and the associated results documented in this thesis are part of the research project Health-e-Child (www.health-e-child.org). The Health-e-Child Project is embedded in the European Union's sixth framework program (FP6) that aims to improve integration and coordination of research within the European Union. Health-e-Child (project identifier: IST-2004-027749) is scheduled from 01/01/2006 to 12/31/2009.

The project's vision is the development of an integrated healthcare platform for European pediatrics that provides seamless integration of traditional and emerging sources of biomedical information. In the long run, Health-e-Child wants to provide access to biomedical knowledge repositories for personalized and preventive healthcare, for large-scale information-based biomedical research and training, and for informed policy making. For the beginning the project focus will be on individualized disease prevention, screening, early diagnosis, therapy and follow-up of three representative pediatric diseases selected from the following three major categories: heart diseases, inflammatory diseases, and brain tumors. By building a European network of leading clinical centers it will be possible to share and annotate biomedical data, validate systems clinically, and diffuse clinical excellence across Europe by setting up new technologies, clinical workflows, and standards. Health-e-Child's key concept is the vertical and longitudinal integration of information across all information layers of biomedical abstraction, that is to say, genetic, cell, tissue, organ, individual and population layer, to provide a unified view of a person's biomedical and clinical condition. This will enable sophisticated knowledge discovery and decision support.

It is intended to integrate diagnostically relevant knowledge and data from multiple sources with radiological imaging being one of them. In order to address this particular part dealing with radiological images of the broader complex of themes within Health-e-Child our research activities aim for providing explicit semantics for medical imaging data by means of medical image segmentation and labeling as mentioned above. These semantics can then be used for multiple purposes, for example, for traditional medical decision making, such as diagnostics and therapy planning and control, as input to computer-aided diagnosis (CAD) systems, for morphological studies, for image enhancement, and in general as input to any system aiming for semantic data integration.

1.6   Contributions

Contributions to the scientific progress could be made in all medical image segmentation scenarios addressed by this thesis. They can be summarized as follows:

- For the first scenario we introduce a novel fully automated method for brain tissue classification, that is, segmentation into cerebral GM, cerebral WM, and CSF, and intra-scan INU correction in 3-D MR images.

- For the second scenario we present a novel fully automated approach to pediatric brain tumor segmentation in multi-spectral 3-D MR images.

- For the third scenario we introduce a novel method for the automatic detection and segmentation of (sub-)cortical GM structures in 3-D MR images based on the recently introduced concept of marginal space learning (MSL).

- As a minor contribution we adapt a dynamic programming approach for 1-D histogram matching to mono-spectral MRI inter-scan intensity standardization in the second and third scenario. We give a graph theoretic re-formulation of the algorithm and extend it to minimize the Kullback-Leibler divergence instead of the histograms' sum of squared differences. This necessary pre-processing step allows us to make use of machine learning methods relying on intensity-based features in the context of MRI.

1.7 Outline

In the following chapter, that is, **Chapter 2**, we describe our novel fully automated method for brain tissue classification and intra-scan INU correction in 3-D MR images. It combines supervised MRI modality-specific discriminative modeling and unsupervised statistical expectation maximization (EM) segmentation into an integrated Bayesian framework. The Markov random field (MRF) regularization involved takes into account knowledge about spatial and appearance related homogeneity of segments and patient-specific knowledge about the global spatial distribution of brain tissue. It is based on a strong discriminative model provided by a probabilistic boosting-tree (PBT) for classifying image voxels. It relies on surrounding context and alignment-based features derived from a probabilistic anatomical atlas. The context considered is encoded by 3-D Haar-like features of reduced INU sensitivity. Detailed quantitative evaluations on standard phantom scans and standard real world data show the accuracy and robustness of the proposed method. They also demonstrate relative superiority in comparison with other state-of-the-art approaches to this kind of computational task.

Chapter 3 details on our novel fully automated approach to pediatric brain tumor segmentation in multi-spectral 3-D MR images. It is a top-down segmentation approach based on an MRF model that combines PBTs and low-level segmentation via graph cuts. The PBT algorithm provides a strong discriminative prior model that classifies tumor appearance while a spatial prior takes into account pair-wise voxel homogeneities in terms of classification labels and multi-spectral voxel intensities. The discriminative model relies not only on observed local intensities but also on surrounding context for detecting candidate regions for pathology. A mathematically sound formulation for integrating the two approaches into a unified statistical framework is given. The results obtained in a quantitative evaluation are mostly better than those reported for current state-of-the-art approaches to 3-D MRI brain tumor segmentation.

Chapter 4 introduces a novel method for the automatic detection and segmentation of (sub-)cortical GM structures in 3-D MR images of the human brain. The method is a top-down segmentation approach based on the recently introduced concept of MSL [130, 131]. It is shown that MSL naturally decomposes the parameter space of anatomy shapes along decreasing levels of geometrical abstraction into subspaces of increasing dimensionality by exploiting parameter invariance. This allows us to build strong discriminative models from annotated training data on each level of abstraction, and to use these models to narrow the range of possible solutions until a final shape can be inferred. The segmentation accuracy achieved is mostly better than the one of other state-of-the-art approaches using standardized distance and overlap accuracy metrics. For benchmarking, the method is evaluated on two publicly available gold standard databases consisting in total of 42 T1-weighted 3-D brain MRI scans from different scanners and sites.

Chapter 5 concludes the thesis and summarizes its main contributions. We discuss technological and methodological aspects of our work and give an outlook on future research directions with regards to the chosen scenarios. Finally, we name challenges medical image segmentation and understanding faces in order to be of continuous value in today's increasingly cross-linked medical environment and infrastructure.

Chapter 2

3-D MRI Brain Tissue Classification and INU Correction

In this chapter we describe a fully automated method for brain tissue classification, which is the segmentation into cerebral GM, cerebral WM, and CSF, and INU correction in brain MRI volumes. It combines supervised MRI modality-specific discriminative modeling and unsupervised statistical EM segmentation into an integrated Bayesian framework. While both the parametric observation models as well as the non-parametrically modeled INUs are estimated via EM during segmentation itself, an MRF prior model regularizes segmentation and parameter estimation. Firstly, the regularization takes into account knowledge about spatial and appearance related homogeneity of segments in terms of pair-wise clique potentials of adjacent voxels. Secondly and more importantly, patient-specific knowledge about the global spatial distribution of brain tissue is incorporated into the segmentation process via unary clique potentials. They are based on a strong discriminative model provided by a PBT for classifying image voxels. It relies on surrounding context and alignment-based features derived from a probabilistic anatomical atlas. The context considered is encoded by 3-D Haar-like features of reduced INU sensitivity. Alignment is carried out fully automatically by means of an affine registration algorithm minimizing cross-correlation. Both types of features do not immediately use the observed intensities provided by the MRI modality but instead rely on specifically transformed features, which are less sensitive to MRI artifacts. Detailed quantitative evaluations on standard phantom scans and standard real world data show the accuracy and robustness of the proposed method. They also demonstrate relative superiority in comparison to other state-of-the-art approaches to this kind of computational task: our method achieves average Dice coefficients of 0.94 ± 0.02 (WM) and 0.92 ± 0.04 (GM) on simulated mono-spectral and 0.93 ± 0.02 (WM) and 0.91 ± 0.04 (GM) on simulated multi-spectral data from the Brain-Web repository. The scores are 0.81 ± 0.09 (WM) and 0.82 ± 0.06 (GM) and 0.87 ± 0.05 (WM) and 0.83 ± 0.12 (GM) for the two real-world data sets—consisting of 20 and 18

13

patient volumes, respectively—provided by the Internet Brain Segmentation Repository. Preliminary results have been published in reference [125].

2.1   Motivation

Several inquiries in medical diagnostics, therapy planning and monitoring, as well as in medical research, require highly accurate and reproducible brain tissue segmentation in 3-D MRI. For instance, studies of neurodegenerative and psychiatric diseases often rely on quantitative measures obtained from MRI scans that are segmented into the three common tissue types present in the human brain: cerebral GM, cerebral WM, and CSF. There is a need for fully automatic segmentation tools providing reproducible results in this particular context as manual interaction for this type of volumetric labeling is typically considered unacceptable for the following reasons: having 3-D scans manually annotated by radiologists may notably delay clinical workflow, and the annotations obtained may vary significantly among experts as a result of individual experience and interpretation. The mentioned automatic tools face a challenging segmentation task due to the characteristic artifacts of the MRI modality, such as intra-/inter-scan INU [119, 60], partial volume effects (PVE) [114], and Rician noise [80]. The human brain's complexity in shape and natural intensity variations additionally complicate the segmentation task at hand. Once a sufficiently good segmentation is achieved it can also be used in enhancing the image quality, as intra-scan INUs can be easily estimated due to the knowledge of the tissue type and the associated image intensities to be observed at a specific spatial site [119]. As can be seen later there are several interleaved approaches similar to our contribution following this idea where the tissue segmentation and the INU are estimated simultaneously.

The extended hidden Markov random field expectation maximization (HMRF-EM) approach with simultaneous INU correction presented here is, in contrast to Zhang et al. [129][1] , consistently formulated to work on multi-spectral 3-D brain MRI data. Further, we present a mathematically sound integration of prior knowledge encoded by a strong discriminative model into the statistical framework. The learning-based component, that is, a PBT [108], providing the discriminative model exclusively relies on features of reduced sensitivity to INUs and therefore makes this approach MRI modality-specific. Usually, more discriminative features are used for medical image segmentation by means of discriminative PBT modeling, for instance, in CT data [111]. However, those features do not take into account the particularities of the MRI modality, which makes them less suited for MR image segmentation. Approaching the problem this way neglects the fact that relying

---

[1]Although not detailed in the original publication a multi-spectral implementation of Zhang et al.'s method [129] already exists and can be downloaded from www.fmrib.ox.ac.uk/fsl.

on modality-specific features can significantly increase segmentation accuracy in certain cases. [97, 98]

Exhaustive quantitative evaluations on publicly available simulated and real world MRI scans show the relative superiority with regards to robustness of our newly proposed method in comparison to other state-of-the-art approaches [94, 6, 13, 93, 2, 1, 5, 4, 74, 129, 113]. While other methods may reach particular high values on a particular database we present comparable and mostly better results in terms of segmentation accuracy on a variety of benchmarking databases from different sources. This demonstrates the increased robustness of our approach.

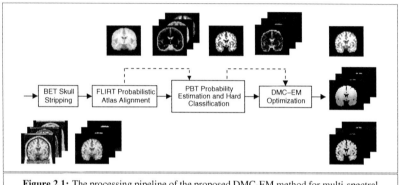

Figure 2.1: The processing pipeline of the proposed DMC-EM method for multi-spectral brain tissue segmentation and INU correction.

Our method consists of four steps: first, the whole brain is extracted from its surroundings with the Brain Extraction Tool (BET) [100] working on the T1-weighted pulse sequence. As BET skull stripping fails on some of the data sets we use for evaluation we extended the original preprocessing tool BET. We introduced thresholding for background exclusion, morphological operations and connected component analysis to generate initializations (center and radius of initial sphere) for the BET main procedure that are closer to the intra-cranial surface to be computed. Then, an initial spatially variant prior of the brain soft tissue on different tissue classes is obtained by means of a strong modality specific discriminative model, that is to say, a PBT probability estimator. This also gives an initial segmentation of the brain soft tissue. Subsequently, the final segmentation and the multi-spectral INU fields are estimated via an extended HMRF-EM approach that operates on multi-spectral input data. We will refer to our method as the discriminative model-constrained HMRF-EM approach (DMC-EM). The whole processing pipeline is depicted in Fig. 2.1.

2.2   Related Work

2.2.1   MRI Tissue Classification

Most approaches in the field of MRI brain tissue segmentation are based on Bayesian modeling, which typically involves providing a prior model and a generative observation model. With these models the most likely tissue class being responsible for the observed intensity values at a certain voxel can be inferred. Offline generated observation models, that is, models generated from annotated training data, usually are very sensitive to MRI artifacts. [54] For this reason parametric models are typically estimated online, that is, simultaneously with an associated segmentation maximizing an a posteriori probability distribution density by means of EM [13, 94, 93, 4, 86, 37, 129, 113, 62, 119]. Apart from EM optimization methods comprise max-flow/min-cut computation [102, 101], segmentation by weighted aggregation [2], and finding the maximizer of the posterior marginals (MPM) in a maximum a posteriori (MAP) setting [74]. Recently also non-parametric [2] approaches for generating observation models within Bayesian frameworks and entirely learning-based [1] approaches to brain tissue classification have been proposed. Some of them [1, 2] do not take into account INUs and scanner-specific contrast characteristics present in the data sets used for model generation, which may result in model over-fitting and poor generalization capabilities.

Commonly used prior models comprise, next to the assumption of spatially uniform prior probabilities, spatial interdependencies among neighboring voxels through prior probabilities modeled as hidden Markov random fields (HMRF) [94, 93, 74, 129, 62], hidden Markov chains (HMC) [13], or non-parametric adaptive Markov priors [5]. They are sometimes combined with prior probabilities derived from probabilistic or anatomical atlases [5, 74, 86, 113] or replaced by them [6, 4] that can also be integrated into the overall MRF-based formulation as external field energies [94, 86]. The same holds for prior knowledge encoded by fuzzy localization maps [93] that can also be integrated into the overall framework via external fields. Alignment of the atlas can be achieved either by rigid [6, 113], affine [94, 2, 5], or non-rigid [13, 74, 86] registration algorithms, either before optimization or simultaneously [6, 4]. Bazin and Pham [6] additionally incorporate prior knowledge obtained from a topological atlas into a fuzzy classification technique for topology preservation. Cuadra et al. [30] compare and validate different statistical non-supervised brain tissue classification techniques in MRI volumes.

Conceptually, our approach aligns with the mentioned EM-based approaches using Markov random field priors and aligned probabilistic atlases. In contrast, though, our method makes use of more general prior knowledge in terms of a strong discriminative model initializing and continually constraining the segmentation process. It is motivated by recent advances in medical image segmentation that make use of prior knowledge in a similar manner, i.e., in terms of discriminative modeling, to improve segmentation accuracy and robustness [121, 77, 21, 28, 111]. We have chosen the PBT algorithm for discriminative modeling as it has been found to perform well in a variety of medical imaging settings [126, 77, 121, 111, 19, 131].

In many cases the related approaches completely lack a quantitative evaluation [129] or are exclusively quantitatively validated on synthetic data [94, 93, 4]. In other cases quantitative evaluation is carried out only on a small collection of scans from a single source of data [13, 38, 1, 2, 119]. All this imposes a restriction on the generalization capabilities of such methods.

2.2.2 MRI INU Correction

While some of the papers mentioned above address further segmentation of cerebral gray matter into individual structures [94, 93, 2, 6], which is beyond the scope of this chapter, only some of them additionally address INU correction [13, 101, 102, 4, 129, 113, 119]. INUs are usually modeled as multiplicative noise corrupting the images in the intensity domain and as additive noise in the log-domain. They can be described either non-parametrically as bias or gain fields in the literal sense [129, 119] or parametrically by polynomial basis functions [13, 112], by means of cubic B-splines [102, 101] or through the exponential of a linear combination of low frequency basis functions [4]. Other approaches rely on segmentation methods but focus on INU correction [112, 53]. Vovk et al. [116] recently reviewed most of the relevant data-driven approaches in the field including non-segmentation-based approaches like the well-known nonparametric nonuniform intensity normalization (N3) [99] and homomorphic unsharp masking (HUM) [14]. Another detailed review can be found in reference [7]. As we consider INU correction to be a possible application of our novel segmentation approach but not the main focus of our contribution we refer the reader to the reviews mentioned for further information.

2.3 Method

2.3.1 DMC-EM Brain Tissue Segmentation

Image or volume segmentation by means of the DMC-EM approach, which extends the HMRF-EM approach of Zhang et al. [129], is closely related to learning finite Gaussian mixtures (FGM) via the EM algorithm. For both cases let $\mathcal{S} = \{1, 2, \ldots, N\}$, $N \in \mathbb{N}$, be a set of indices to image voxels. At each index $s \in \mathcal{S}$ there are two random variables Y_s and $\boldsymbol{X}_s$ that take discrete values $y_s \in \mathcal{Y} = \{1, \ldots, K\}$, $K \in \mathbb{N}$, and $\boldsymbol{x}_s \in \mathcal{X} = \{1, \ldots, 2^d\}^L$. The former, Y_s, denotes the hidden class label, that is, the underlying tissue class, at voxel s, whereas the latter, $\boldsymbol{X}_s$, states the vector of observed intensity values taken from the

$L \in \mathbb{N}$ aligned input pulse sequences each having a bit depth of $d \in \mathbb{N}$. The observable intensities at every voxel s are assumed to be causally linked to the underlying class labels by parameterized Gaussian distribution densities $p(\boldsymbol{x}_s|y_s = k) = N(\boldsymbol{x}_s; \boldsymbol{\theta}_k)$ with class specific parameters $\boldsymbol{\theta}_k = (\boldsymbol{\mu}_k, \Sigma_k)$, $\boldsymbol{\mu}_k \in \mathbb{R}^L$, $\Sigma_k \in \mathbb{R}^{L \times L}$ and symmetric positive-definite. Starting from initial values for those parameters and some prior probabilities $p^{(0)}(k)$ for the occurrence of each class label a proper statistical model in terms of prior probabilities $p(k)$, $k \in \mathcal{Y}$, and parameters $\Theta = (\boldsymbol{\theta}_k)_{k \in \mathcal{Y}}$ can be estimated by means of EM iteratively in an unsupervised manner.

In contrast to the FGM model that considers every voxel's classification isolated from its local neighborhood the DMC-EM model assumes external influences and spatial inter-dependencies among neighboring voxels. Both can be incorporated into the existing model by describing the family $\boldsymbol{Y} = (Y_s)_{s \in \mathcal{S}}$ of unknown class labels as an MRF. According to Li [69], within an MRF every voxel at index s is associated with a subset $\mathcal{N}_s \subseteq \mathcal{S} \setminus \{s\}$ of neighboring indices having the properties $s \notin \mathcal{N}_s$ and $s \in \mathcal{N}_t \Leftrightarrow t \in \mathcal{N}_s$ for all $s, t \in \mathcal{S}$. The family of random variables $\boldsymbol{Y}$ is said to form an MRF on $\mathcal{S}$ with respect to the neighborhood system $\mathcal{N} = \{\mathcal{N}_s \mid s \in \mathcal{S}\}$ if and only if $p(\boldsymbol{y}) > 0$ for all possible configurations $\boldsymbol{y} = (y_s)_{s \in \mathcal{S}}$, and $p(y_s|(y_t)_{t \in \mathcal{S} \setminus \{s\}}) = p(y_s|\boldsymbol{y}_{\mathcal{N}_s})$ for all $s \in \mathcal{S}$. They are called the positivity property and the Markov property of the MRF.

The graph $G = (V, E)$ with vertices $V = \{v_s \mid s \in \mathcal{S}\}$ and edges $E = \{(v_s, v_t) \mid s \in \mathcal{S}, t \in \mathcal{N}_s\}$ associated with an MRF contains multiple sets of cliques, which are sets of complete sub-graphs, $\mathcal{C}_n$ denoting all the sets of vertices' indices within cliques of size $n \in \{1, \ldots, |V|\}$.

Under these circumstances, according to the Hammersley-Clifford theorem, the joint probability density function (PDF) $p(\boldsymbol{y})$ can equivalently be described by a Gibbs distribution $p(\boldsymbol{y}) = \frac{1}{Z} \exp(-U(\boldsymbol{y}))$. Here $U(\boldsymbol{y}) = \sum_n \sum_{c_n \in \mathcal{C}_n} V_{c_n}(\boldsymbol{y})$ denotes the energy function, which is a sum of clique potentials V_{c_n}, and $Z = \sum_{\boldsymbol{y}} \exp(-U(\boldsymbol{y}))$ denotes the partition function, which is a normalization constant.

In contrast to Zhang et al. [129] our model considers both unary ($n = 1$) as well as pair-wise ($n = 2$) clique potentials as we want to introduce an MRF prior that constrains segmentation by an external field, provided by a strong discriminative model, and by mutual spatial dependencies among pairs of neighboring voxels. In this case the energy function can be stated as

$$U(\boldsymbol{y}) = \sum_{s \in \mathcal{S}} \left(V_s(y_s) + \frac{\beta}{2} \sum_{t \in \mathcal{N}_s} V_{st}(y_s, y_t) \right). \tag{2.1}$$

For the purpose of image segmentation it is common practice [30, 129] to ignore further dependencies, i.e., higher-ordered clique potentials. These potentials increase the degrees of freedom of the MRF and therefore require more training data for reliable parameter estimation. Thus, by applying Bayes' rule and by marginalizing over the possible class labels, we have

$$
\begin{aligned}
p(y_s|\boldsymbol{y}_{\mathcal{N}_s}) &= p(y_s|(y_t)_{t\in\mathcal{S}\setminus\{s\}}) \\
&= \frac{p(y_s,(y_t)_{t\in\mathcal{S}\setminus\{s\}})}{\sum_{k\in\mathcal{Y}} p(y_s = k,(y_t)_{t\in\mathcal{S}\setminus\{s\}})} \\
&= \frac{\exp(-V_s(y_s) - \sum_{t\in\mathcal{N}_s} V_{st}(y_s,y_t))}{\sum_{k\in\mathcal{Y}} \exp(-V_s(y_s = k) - \sum_{t\in\mathcal{N}_s} V_{st}(y_s = k,y_t))}
\end{aligned}
\tag{2.2}
$$

with the labels $\boldsymbol{y}_{\mathcal{N}_s}$ understood as observable evidence.

Due to the fact that Equation (2.2) can be formulated dependent on unary and pair-wise clique potentials it is possible to introduce prior knowledge into the classification process. In order to make a strong discriminative model constrain expectation maximization we will later define unary clique potentials based on tissue class probability estimations from PBT classifiers. With regards to the pair-wise clique potentials, which are defined on fully labeled data, the best segmentation $\arg\max_{\boldsymbol{y}} p(\boldsymbol{y}|\boldsymbol{x};\Theta^{(i-1)})$ that is needed to properly evaluate $V_{st}(y_s,y_t)$ in iteration i is not available during iterative expectation maximization. This means, in accordance with Zhang et al. [129], a currently best segmentation using the MAP

$$
\boldsymbol{y}^* = \arg\max_{\boldsymbol{y}} p(\boldsymbol{y}|\boldsymbol{x};\Theta^{(i-1)})
\tag{2.3}
$$

where

$$
\begin{aligned}
p(\boldsymbol{y}|\boldsymbol{x};\Theta^{(i-1)}) &= \frac{p(\boldsymbol{x}|\boldsymbol{y};\Theta^{(i-1)})p(\boldsymbol{y})}{p(\boldsymbol{x})} \\
&= \frac{1}{Z}\prod_s \frac{p(\boldsymbol{x}_s|y_s;\boldsymbol{\theta}^{(i-1)})\cdot\exp(-V_s(y_s) - \sum_{t\in\mathcal{N}_s} V_{st}(y_s,y_t))}{p(\boldsymbol{x}_s)} \\
&\propto \prod_s N(\boldsymbol{x}_s|\boldsymbol{\theta}^{(i-1)})\cdot\exp(-V_s(y_s) - \sum_{t\in\mathcal{N}_s} V_{st}(y_s,y_t))
\end{aligned}
\tag{2.4}
$$

has to be found in every iteration i of the overall expectation maximization procedure to form the complete dataset where we assume the intensities $\boldsymbol{X}_s$ to be i.i.d. In our method forming the complete dataset is done by iterated conditional modes (ICM) as proposed by Besag [9] and adapted for brain tissue segmentation by Zhang et al. [129]. Alternatives for this processing step include optimization via multi-class generalized max-flow/min-cut algorithms. The two-class base algorithms of this nature will be discussed in more detail in Chapter 3.

Once a sufficiently good approximation of the currently best segmentation is computed the parameters of the intensity model can be updated by

$$\boldsymbol{\mu}_k^{(t)} = \frac{\sum_{s \in \mathcal{S}} p(y_s = k | \boldsymbol{x}_s, \boldsymbol{y}_{\mathcal{N}_s}; \boldsymbol{\theta}_k^{(t-1)}) \boldsymbol{x}_s}{\sum_{s \in \mathcal{S}} p(y_s = k | \boldsymbol{x}_s, \boldsymbol{y}_{\mathcal{N}_s}; \boldsymbol{\theta}_k^{(t-1)})} \tag{2.5}$$

and

$$\boldsymbol{\Sigma}_k^{(t)} = \frac{\sum_{s \in \mathcal{S}} p(y_s = k | \boldsymbol{x}_s, \boldsymbol{y}_{\mathcal{N}_s}; \boldsymbol{\theta}_k^{(t-1)})(\boldsymbol{x}_s - \boldsymbol{\mu}_k^{(t)})(\boldsymbol{x}_s - \boldsymbol{\mu}_k^{(t)})^T}{\sum_{s \in \mathcal{S}} p(y_s = k | \boldsymbol{x}_s, \boldsymbol{y}_{\mathcal{N}_s}; \boldsymbol{\theta}_k^{(t-1)})}. \tag{2.6}$$

It has to be mentioned that this so-called Besag pseudo-likelihood approach [113] that relies on an approximation of a complete labeling is only one of a variety of sometimes more principled approaches addressing the entire EM parameter update with a unified optimization strategy. Alternative methods allow "fuzzy" class-memberships and handle the spatial priors directly by other numerical maximizations methods such as mean field-like approximations [128, 62, 112] or non-iterative heuristic approaches [113]. We refer to Marroquin et al. [74] for a more detailed discussion of the possible design choices concerning this step within the overall procedure.

The complete DMC-EM procedure can be summarized as follows: starting from initial values $\boldsymbol{y}^{(0)}$ and $\Theta^{(0)}$, in each iteration i the current segmentation $\boldsymbol{y}^{(i)}$ is approximated and used to compute the posterior probabilities $p(y_s = k | \boldsymbol{x}_s, \boldsymbol{y}_{\mathcal{N}_s}; \boldsymbol{\theta}_k^{(i-1)})$ for each voxel $s \in \mathcal{S}$. Subsequently, the parameters $\Theta^{(i)}$ are updated.

At this current point our method equals the HMRF-EM approach [129]. In the following sections we will derive unary and pair-wise clique potentials that take into account probability estimations from a strong MRI modality-specific discriminative model, i.e. a PBT, and spatial coherence in terms of observed intensities and current classification labels, respectively. This combination of discriminative modeling via the PBT algorithm and MAP tissue classification via the EM algorithm through the formulation of appropriate unary clique potentials is what we consider the major contribution of our work. It is also what makes the difference between our DMC-EM algorithm and the HMRF-EM algorithm [129]. Further we will extend the approach from its theoretical point of view in order to simultaneously estimate multi-spectral INUs similarly to Zhang et al. [129] who presented a mono-spectral extension of their method for this purpose.

2.3.2   MRI INU Estimation

As shown by Zhang et al. [129] the HMRF-EM as well as our DMC-EM method can easily be extended to simultaneously estimate the INU field according to the method of Wells et al. [119]. The INUs are modeled by a multiplicative gain field $\boldsymbol{g} = (g_s)_{s \in \mathcal{S}}$ that disturbs the true intensities $\boldsymbol{i}^* = (i_s^*)_{s \in \mathcal{S}}$. That is

$$i_s = i_s^* \cdot g_s \tag{2.7}$$

for one of the MRI channels at voxel $s \in \mathcal{S}$ where $\boldsymbol{i} = (i_s)_{s \in \mathcal{S}}$ are the disturbed and observed intensities. Although less appropriate for modeling INUs caused by induced currents and inhomogeneous excitation within the acquisition device the multiplicative model adequately describes the inhomogeneous sensitivity of the reception coil. [99] After logarithmic transformation of intensities the gain field can be treated as an additive bias field $\boldsymbol{b} = (b_s)_{s \in \mathcal{S}}$ and

$$x_s = x_s^* + b_s, \tag{2.8}$$

where $x_s = \ln(i_s)$, $x_s^* = \ln(i_s^*)$, and $b_s = \ln(g_s)$. In the case of multi-spectral images we have

$$\boldsymbol{x}_s = \boldsymbol{x}_s^* + \boldsymbol{b}_s. \tag{2.9}$$

For DMC-EM this means that the class-conditional probabilities are no longer only dependent on the parameters Θ of the Gaussian distributions but also of the bias field $\boldsymbol{b}$, that is,

$$p(\boldsymbol{x}_s|y_s, \boldsymbol{b}_s) = N(\boldsymbol{x}_s - \boldsymbol{b}_s; \boldsymbol{\theta}_k). \tag{2.10}$$

Following Wells et al. [119] the joint probability of intensities and tissue class conditioned on the bias field can be stated as

$$p(\boldsymbol{x}_s, y_s|\boldsymbol{b}_s) = p(\boldsymbol{x}_s|y_s, \boldsymbol{b}_s)p(y_s). \tag{2.11}$$

Marginalization over $\mathcal{Y}$ yields

$$p(\boldsymbol{x}_s|\boldsymbol{b}_s) = \sum_{k \in \mathcal{Y}} p(\boldsymbol{x}_s|y_s = k, \boldsymbol{b}_s)p(y_s = k), \tag{2.12}$$

which is a class-independent PDF consisting of a mixture of Gaussian populations. By applying the MAP principle to the posterior probability of the bias field, which can be derived from Equation (2.12), an initial expression for the bias field estimate can be formulated. Then, a zero-gradient condition with respect to $\boldsymbol{b}$ leads to a non-linear bias field estimator fulfilling a necessary condition for optimality:

$$\boldsymbol{b} = \left[\overline{\Sigma^{-1}} + \Sigma_b^{-1} \right]^{-1} \overline{\boldsymbol{r}}, \tag{2.13}$$

where $\bar{r} = (\bar{r}_s)_{s \in \mathcal{S}}$ are the mean residuals

$$\bar{r}_s = \sum_{k \in \mathcal{Y}} p(y_s = k | \boldsymbol{x}_s, \boldsymbol{b}_s)(\boldsymbol{x}_s - \boldsymbol{\mu}_k)^T \Sigma_k^{-1} (\boldsymbol{x}_s - \boldsymbol{\mu}_k) \tag{2.14}$$

and $\overline{\Sigma^{-1}} = (\overline{\Sigma^{-1}}_s)_{s \in \mathcal{S}}$ are the mean inverse covariances with entries

$$\overline{\Sigma^{-1}}_s = \sum_{k \in \mathcal{Y}} p(y_s = k | \boldsymbol{x}_s, \boldsymbol{b}_s) \Sigma_k^{-1} \tag{2.15}$$

written down as a family of $L \times L$ matrices. Please refer to Wells et al. [119] for a detailed description of the mathematical assumptions and derivation steps involved.

Using an approximation instead of the optimal estimator the bias field at every voxel $s \in \mathcal{S}$ is given by

$$\boldsymbol{b}_s = \left(\mathbf{F}[\overline{\Sigma^{-1}}] \right)_s^{-1} \cdot (\mathbf{F}[\overline{r}])_s \tag{2.16}$$

where $\mathbf{F}$ is a low-pass filter working component-wise on the matrix- or vector-valued, in our case, volumes $\bar{r}$ and $\overline{\Sigma^{-1}}$ [118].

The DMC-EM algorithm for simultaneous brain tissue segmentation and INU correction of multi-spectral data with a predefined number T of iterations can be stated as depicted in Algorithm 1. In accordance with Zhang et al. [129] the parameter update is consistently based on the original, non-corrected data such that the complete bias field can be estimated appropriately in each iteration.

As pointed out by Zhang et al. [129] and originally discovered by Guillemaud and Brady [53] the method of Wells et al. [119], which serves as the base of our INU correction system, does not adequately work on image segments whose actual intensity distribution is not Gaussian. Such a tissue class usually has a large variance, which prevents the mean from being representative. In our system this is the case for the CSF tissue class that does not only include the ventricular system inside but also around the brain. Especially at the outer bounds of the automatically generated brain mask, this class may include several other non-brain structures introducing intensity values different from the ones expected from true CSF, which correspondingly increases intra-class variance. Inspired by Wells et al. [119], where everything but GM and WM is excluded both from the INU estimation as well as from the segmentation, we therefore estimate the bias field only on the current GM and WM segments assuming the current CSF segment to be part of the background. However, in contrast to Wells et al. [119], we do address CSF segmentation, together with GM and WM segmentation, during iterative tissue classification.

In the following we will derive appropriate higher dimensional feature vectors $\boldsymbol{z}$ for PBT training and PBT probability estimation. In order to keep the discriminative models MRI modality-specific we have to make sure that the features $\boldsymbol{z}$ used are not sensitive to inter- and intra-scan INUs as probability estimation will be performed on the non-corrected

---

Algorithm 1: DMC-EM algorithm

Input: (Multi-spectral) MRI volume x, parameters $\Theta^{(0)} = (\theta_k^{(0)} = (\boldsymbol{\mu}_k^{(0)}, \boldsymbol{\Sigma}_k^{(0)}))_{k \in \mathcal{Y}}$, initial
    segmentation $y^{(0)}$
Output: Parameters $\Theta^{(t)}$, segmentation $y^{(t)}$, and bias field $b^{(t)}$
begin
    $t \leftarrow 0$;
    $\Theta^{(t)} \leftarrow \Theta^{(0)}$;
    $b^{(t)} \leftarrow 0$;
    repeat
        $t \leftarrow t + 1$;

        // 1. Estimate the class labels by MRF-MAP estimation (see Equation (2.3))
        $y^{(t)} \leftarrow \arg\max_y p(y|x; \Theta^{(t-1)}, b)$;

        // 2. Calculate the posterior distributions for the corrected and non-corrected intensities
        forall *voxels* s **do**
            forall *class labels* k **do**

$$p(y_s = k|x_s, y_{\mathcal{N}_s}, \theta_k^{(t-1)}, b_s) \leftarrow \frac{N(x_s - b_s; \theta_k^{(t-1)})p(y_s = k|y_{\mathcal{N}_s})}{\sum_{l \in \mathcal{Y}} N(x_s - b_s; \theta_l^{(t-1)})p(y_s = l|y_{\mathcal{N}_s})};$$

$$p(y_s = k|x_s, y_{\mathcal{N}_s}; \theta_k^{(t-1)}) \leftarrow \frac{N(x_s; \theta_k^{(t-1)})p(y_s = k|y_{\mathcal{N}_s})}{\sum_{l \in \mathcal{Y}} N(x_s; \theta_l^{(t-1)})p(y_s = l|y_{\mathcal{N}_s})};$$

            end
        end

        // 3. Update the parameters of the observation model (see Equations (2.5) and (2.6))
$$\boldsymbol{\mu}_k^{(t)} \leftarrow \frac{\sum_{s \in S} p(y_s = k|x_s, y_{\mathcal{N}_s}; \theta_k^{(t-1)})x_s}{\sum_{s \in S} p(y_s = k|x_s, y_{\mathcal{N}_s}; \theta_k^{(t-1)})};$$

$$\boldsymbol{\Sigma}_k^{(t)} \leftarrow \frac{\sum_{s \in S} p(y_s = k|x_s, y_{\mathcal{N}_s}; \theta_k^{(t-1)})(x_s - \boldsymbol{\mu}^{(t)})(x_s - \boldsymbol{\mu}^{(t)})^T}{\sum_{s \in S} p(y_s = k|x_s, y_{\mathcal{N}_s}; \theta_k^{(t-1)})};$$

        // 4. Estimate the bias field (see Equation (2.16))
        forall *voxels* s **do**
$$b_s = \left[\mathbf{F}(\overline{\boldsymbol{\Sigma}^{-1}})\right]_s^{-1} \cdot [\mathbf{F}\overline{r}]_s;$$
        end
    until $t=T$;
end

---

input data. We will therefore rely on 3-D Haar-like [111] features of reduced INU sensitivity and probabilistic atlas-based whole brain anatomy features. Both types of features are the result of specific transformations and do not immediately use the observed intensities provided by the MRI modality.

2.3.3 MRI Modality-Specific Discriminative Model-Based Unary Clique Potentials

Probabilistic Boosting-Tree

The discriminative classifier PBT [108] recursively groups boosted ensembles of weak classifiers to a tree structure during learning from expert annotated data (see Appendix A).

For every tissue class we learn a voxel-wise discriminative PBT probability estimator relying on higher dimensional feature vectors z_s, which are derived from the surrounding 3-D context of a voxel of interest s. We use the class-wise probability estimates $\tilde{p}^k(+1|z_s)$, $k \in \{1, \ldots, K\}$, for the K tissue classes to define the unary clique potentials

$$V_s(y_s = k) = -\ln \tilde{p}^k(+1|z_s) \tag{2.17}$$

used in our system.

Haar-like Features of Reduced INU Sensitivity

In the case of a 1-D signal $f(t)$, $t \in \mathbb{R}$, as well as for any higher dimensional signal Haar-like filters can be interpreted as non-normalized child wavelets $\psi(\frac{t-\tau}{\alpha})$ of the classical Haar mother wavelet

$$\psi(t) = \begin{cases} 1 & \text{if } 0 \leq t < \frac{1}{2}, \\ -1 & \text{if } \frac{1}{2} \leq t < 1, \\ 0 & \text{otherwise.} \end{cases} \tag{2.18}$$

As normalization does not affect linear independence the family of non-normalized child wavelets spans the same infinite-dimensional vector space as their normalized counterparts. Feature responses, which are comparable to wavelet coefficients, typically are only computed for discrete $-\tau_{max} \leq \tau \leq +\tau_{max}$ and $0 < \alpha \leq \alpha_{max}$. This equals projecting a transformed signal to a finite-dimensional subspace where only certain position and frequency characteristics are taken into account. As seen above, MRI inter-scan intensity inhomogeneities can be modeled as gain fields [119] where a spatially varying factor multiplicatively disturbs the observed intensities i_s at voxel $s \in \mathcal{S}$. After logarithmic transformation it can be seen as an additive bias field of low frequency and zero mean. The parameter α_{max} can be chosen sufficiently low such that low frequencies of that kind are attenuated and do not significantly affect the signal's projection onto the subspace. The obtained coefficients are therefore of reduced bias field sensitivity when considering the log-transformed signal and of reduced gain field, that is, INU field, sensitivity in the original domain.

This becomes exemplarily apparent if we consider the Fourier transforms

$$\begin{aligned} \text{FT}\left[\psi\left(\frac{t}{\alpha}\right)\right] &= \text{FT}\left[\text{rect}\left(\frac{2}{\alpha}t - \frac{1}{2}\right) - \text{rect}\left(\frac{2}{\alpha}t - \frac{3}{2}\right)\right] \\ &= \frac{|\alpha|}{2}\,\text{si}\left(f\frac{\alpha}{2}\right)\exp(-i\pi f\frac{\alpha}{2}) \\ &\quad - \frac{|\alpha|}{2}\,\text{si}\left(f\frac{\alpha}{2}\right)\exp(-i\pi f\frac{3\alpha}{2}) \end{aligned} \tag{2.19}$$

of the 1-D Haar-like filters where $\tau = 0$ without loss of generality. The filter states a band-pass filter whose band-width enlarges with increasing α. This observation can be generalized to other additive combinations of rectangular impulses and higher-dimensional signals.

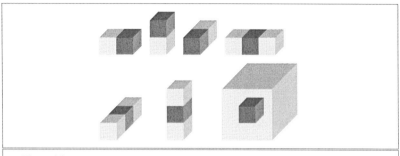

Figure 2.2: The 3-D Haar-like feature prototypes used in the DMC-EM algorithm's discriminative model.

This is perfectly accompanied by the intuition that small neighboring areas should have an almost identical additive bias in the log-domain, which disappears after subtraction when computing the Haar-like features. Fig. 2.2 depicts the 3-D Haar-like feature prototypes used in our system. The associated features are computed at different anisotropic scales of the prototypes with a fixed offset centered at the voxel of interest. For every feature prototype the average of the log-transformed intensities within the white cuboids is subtracted from the average of the log-transformed intensities within the black cuboids.

Probabilistic Atlas-Based Whole Brain Anatomy Features

The second category of features contributing to the feature vectors z_s for PBT training and probability estimation encode the voxel's probability to be either part of the CSF, the GM, or the WM. They are taken from a probabilistic anatomical atlas [91], which is affinely registered [94, 2, 5] with the current patient data set by means of the publicly available registration software FLIRT [61]. The objective function for the registration step is based on the correlation ratio metric, which is suited for inter-modality registration purposes by design. It ensures robustness of the registration procedure in the case of inter- and intra-scan INUs. The choice in favor for a 12-parameter affine registration algorithm is motivated by the trade-off between maximum flexibility and computational demand of the underlying registration procedure. Non-rigid registration algorithms may lead to more discriminative atlas-based features. [13, 4, 74]

2.3.4   Coherence Preserving Pair-wise Clique Potentials

Inspired by Boykov and Funka-Lea [10] the interaction potentials used in our system are

$$V_{st}(y_s, y_t) \propto \exp\left(-\frac{1}{2L}\sum_{l=1}^{L}\frac{(x_{s_l} - x_{t_l})^2}{(\Sigma_{l,l})_{y_s}^{(t)}}\right) \cdot \frac{\delta(y_s, y_t)}{\text{dist}(s, t)} \tag{2.20}$$

where vectors $(x_{s_1}, \ldots, x_{s_L})^T$ and $(x_{t_1}, \ldots, x_{t_L})^T$ denote the observed intensities at voxels s and t taken from $L \in \mathbb{N}$ aligned input pulse sequences and

$$\delta(y_s, y_t) = \begin{cases} 1 & \text{if } y_s \neq y_t, \\ 0 & \text{otherwise.} \end{cases} \tag{2.21}$$

The function $\text{dist}(s, t)$ denotes the physical distance between voxels s and t, which varies when working on image volumes with anisotropic voxel spacing. The model emphasizes homogeneous classifications among neighboring voxels but weights penalties for heterogeneity according to intensity similarities of the voxels involved. It assumes the noise among neighboring voxels of an input volume to be distributed in a multivariate Gaussian manner without taking into account dependencies among the spectral channels. Discontinuities between voxels of similar intensities are penalized if the multi-spectral intensity differences $|x_{s_l} - x_{t_l}|$, $l = 1, \ldots, L$, are on average smaller than the associated standard deviations $\sqrt{(\Sigma_{l,l})_{y_s}^{(t)}}$ of the considered tissue class y_s in iteration t. However, if the multi-spectral voxel intensities are very different, that is to say, the differences $|x_{s_l} - x_{t_l}|$, $l = 1, \ldots, L$, are on average larger than the associated standard deviations $\sqrt{(\Sigma_{l,l})_{y_s}^{(t)}}$ the penalty is small.

2.3.5   Summary

Reconsidering the processing pipeline of our DMC-EM approach depicted in Fig. 1 we make use of the results from the PBT probability estimation and classification step in the subsequent DMC-EM optimization step in two ways: first, we use the PBT hard classification as initial segmentation $y^{(0)}$ where $y_s^{(0)} = \arg\max_k \tilde{p}^k(+1|z_s)$ at the beginning of the EM iterations. Based on this initial hard classification the parameters $\Theta^{(0)}$ are initialized via class-wise maximum likelihood estimation. Second, the probability estimates serve as constraints for the maximization of Equation (2.3) via ICM within every iteration t as well as for the parameter updates given by Equations (2.5) and (2.6). This is achieved by defining the unary clique potentials as functions of the PBT probability estimates in Equation (2.17). We therefore utilize the discriminative model involved not only as a preprocessing step but also throughout the whole optimization procedure to repeatedly regularize model adaptation.

	Multi-spectral BrainWeb	Mono-spectral BrainWeb
Source	www.bic.mni.mcgill.ca/brainweb	www.bic.mni.mcgill.ca/brainweb
Volume Size	$181 \times 217 \times 181$	$181 \times 217 \times 181$
Voxel Spacing	$1.0 \times 1.0 \times 1.0$ mm^3	$1.0 \times 1.0 \times 1.0$ mm^3
Spectral Channels	T1, T2, PD	T1
Number of Scans	10	10

Table 2.1: Summary of the publicly available standard databases from the BrainWeb repository used for evaluation purposes.

2.4 Validation

2.4.1 Experimental Setup

For quantitative evaluation of the proposed method we carried out experiments both on mono-spectral as well as on multi-spectral (T1-weighted, T2-weighted, PD-weighted) publicly available simulated MRI scans from Cocosco et al. [22] (see Table 2.1). All the simulated MRI volume sequences share resolution and size of $1.0 \times 1.0 \times 1.0$ mm^3 and $181 \times 217 \times 181$, respectively. INU and noise levels vary among 20% and 40%, and 1%, 3%, 5%, 7%, and 9%, correspondingly. The noise in the simulated images follows a Rayleigh distribution in the background and a Rician distribution in the signal regions. The noise level represents the percent ratio of the standard deviation of the white Gaussian noise added to the real and imaginary channels during simulation versus a reference tissue intensity.

Furthermore, our system was quantitatively evaluated on two sets of real T1-weighted MRI scans provided by the Center of Morphometric Analysis at the Massachusetts General Hospital (see Table 2.2), which are publicly available on the Internet Brain Segmentation Repository (IBSR). One of the data sets consists of 20 coronal T1-weighted MRI volumes ($256 \times 65 \times 256$) of normal subjects with a resolution of $1.0 \times 3.1 \times 1.0$ mm^3 (IBSR 20). The other one (IBSR 18) consists of 18 scans ($256 \times 256 \times 128$) of normal subjects with varying resolutions ($0.84 \times 0.84 \times 1.5$ mm^3, $0.94 \times 0.94 \times 1.5$ mm^3, and $1.0 \times 1.0 \times 1.5$ mm^3). Both the sets are accompanied by ground-truth segmentations of the three tissue types of interest (CSF, GM, and WM). All the scans had been subject to a specific preprocessing including spatial normalization before they were released in the IBSR. However, our system does not make use of the additional spatial information provided herewith and the scans are treated as if they were native scans according to the common quality standards of radiological image acquisition.

All the images were re-oriented to a uniform orientation ("RAI"; right-to-left, anterior-to-posterior, inferior-to-superior). The discriminative model involved was trained on one volumetric scan of the IBSR 20 data set, which is therefore excluded from the quantitative

	IBSR 18	IBSR 20
Source	www.cma.mgh.harvard.edu/ibsr	www.cma.mgh.harvard.edu/ibsr
Volume Size	$256 \times 256 \times 128$	$256 \times 65 \times 256$
Voxel Spacing	$0.84 \times 0.84 \times 1.5$ mm^3,	$1.0 \times 3.1 \times 1.0$ mm^3
	$0.94 \times 0.94 \times 1.5$ mm^3,	
	$1.0 \times 1.0 \times 1.5$ mm^3	
Spectral Channels	T1	T1
Number of Scans	18	20

Table 2.2: Summary of the publicly available standard databases from the IBSR used for evaluation purposes.

evaluations. In order to keep our system as general as possible, we use the same model for multi-spectral data and carry out PBT probability estimation and hard classification based on the T1-weighted pulse sequences. We measure segmentation accuracy by means of the Dice coefficient and the Jaccard coefficient to ensure comparability to other work (see Tables 2.4–2.7). We refer to Appendix B for details on how both the coefficients are computed. The quality of INU correction is quantified by the class-wise coefficient of variation (COV = standard deviation / average) achieved.

Table 2.3 summarizes the methods whose accuracy will be compared one against the other later. All of them were evaluated on at least one of the publicly available standard databases mentioned above.

Due to the larger amount of free parameters involved, especially with regards to the PBT model, we did not have the ambition to evaluate every possible choice of parameter settings throughout the processing pipeline. For every processing step design choices were based on what can be found in the literature, e.g., [111]. For example, we set the weight of the pair-wise clique potentials $\beta = 1.2$ in accordance with Cuadra et al. [30] whose Potts model-based pair-wise clique potentials have approximately the same range as ours. The PBT voxel classifiers were built from approximately one million samples randomly selected from one training volume. The samples are voxels within the brain of the patients and are uniformly distributed over all the input slices of the training scan. For PBT probability estimation and classifier training the scans were re-sampled to a voxel spacing of $2.0 \times 2.0 \times 2.0$mm^3. The maximum number of features selected by AdaBoost in each tree node was set to 8. The maximum depth of the trees learned was restricted to 10 and a soft thresholding parameter of $\epsilon = 0.05$ was used. The 3-D voxel context chosen for computing the 747 Haar-like features used per individual voxel sample was of size $30 \times 30 \times 30$mm^3 centered at the voxel of interest.

In a standard C++ implementation of our segmentation framework, it takes about 12 minutes to process one mono-spectral MRI volume ($181 \times 217 \times 181$) without brain extraction and affine alignment on a Fujitsu Siemens notebook equipped with an Intel Core

Method	Characteristics	INU correction	Multi-spectral
DMC-EM	Parametric EM-based approach with MRF prior and integrated discriminative model relying on MRI-specific Haar-like features and rigidly aligned probabilistic atlas-based features	Yes	Yes
Awate et al. [5]	Iterative approach with adaptive, non-parametric MRF prior and affinely aligned probabilistic atlas-based initialization and regularization	No	Yes
van Leemput et al. [113]	Parametric EM-based approach with MRF prior, rigidly aligned probabilistic atlas-based initialization and regularization	Yes	Yes
Bazin and Pham [6]	Fuzzy classification approach with rigidly aligned probabilistic and topological atlas-based initialization and simultaneous rigid re-alignment and topology preservation	Yes	Yes
LOCUS-T [93]	Parametric EM-based approach with MRF prior and integrated FLM-based regularization, Fuzzy C-Means initialization and regular image volume decomposition	No	No
FBM-T [94]	Parametric EM-based approach with MRF prior with integrated affinely aligned probabilistic atlas-based initialization and regularization and integrated parameter regularization across image sub-volumes	No	No
Akselrod-Ballin et al. [1]	Support vector machine-based voxel classification relying on intensity, texture, shape, and rigidly aligned probabilistic atlas-based features	No	No
Akselrod-Ballin et al. [2]	Bayesian multiscale segmentation framework with affinely aligned probabilistic atlas-based initialization and regularization and non-parametric tissue class modeling	No	No
HMRF-EM [129]	Parametric EM-based approach with MRF prior with thresholding-based initialization	Yes	No
Bricq et al. [13]	Parametric EM-based approach with HMC prior and non-rigidly aligned probabilistic atlas-based initialization and regularization	Yes	No
Ashburner and Friston [4]	Parametric EM-based approach with simultaneous non-rigid alignment of probabilistic atlas priors for regularization	Yes	No
Marroquin et al. [74]	Parametric MPM-MAP-based approach with MRF prior and non-rigidly aligned probabilistic atlas-based initialization and regularization	Yes	No

Table 2.3: Summary of the methods used for benchmarking.

2 Duo CPU (2.20 GHz) and 3 GB of memory. During all our experiments, mono-spectral and multi-spectral, we keep a uniform parameter setting for all the free parameters involved both for PBT training and probability estimation as well as for DMC-EM optimization. We can therefore exclude over-adaptation to one particular set of MRI scans.

Method	Tissue Class	Dice Coeff.	Jaccard Coeff.
DMC-EM	WM	0.94 ± 0.02	0.89 ± 0.04
	GM	0.92 ± 0.03	0.85 ± 0.06
	CSF	0.77 ± 0.03	0.63 ± 0.03
Marroquin et al. [74]	WM	0.95 ± 0.02	-
	GM	0.94 ± 0.02	-
	CSF	-	-
van Leemput et al. [113]	WM	0.92 ± 0.03	-
	GM	0.93 ± 0.02	-
	CSF	-	-
Bazin and Pham [6]	WM	0.94 ± 0.02	-
	GM	0.92 ± 0.02	-
	CSF	0.92 ± 0.01	-
Awate et al. [5]	WM	0.95 ± 0.01	-
	GM	0.91 ± 0.01	-
	CSF	-	-

Table 2.4: Average segmentation accuracy for multi-spectral (T1-weighted, T2-weighted, and PD-weighted) simulated BrainWeb data of noise levels 1%, 3%, 5%, 7%, and 9%, and INUs of 20% and 40%. From left to right the columns contain the tissue class and the achieved average Dice and Jaccard coefficients.

2.4.2   Quantitative Results on Multi-Spectral Simulated BrainWeb Data

Results on multi-spectral BrainWeb data obtained by DMC-EM are comparable to those of Bazin and Pham [6][2] and van Leemput et al. [113][3] as depicted in Table 2.4. They are close to those of Awate et al. [5][4] and worse than those of Marroquin et al. [74][5]. However, the quantitative results reported in reference [5] might have been subject to a misconception in the used evaluation software as the images presented show obvious segmentation failures at the outer bounds of the brain for one of the BrainWeb data sets (5% noise and 40% bias). For details refer to Awate et al. [5], p. 735, Figs. 1(b) and 1(c). For the sake of a fair comparison it has to be mentioned though that both Awate et al. [5] as well as van Leemput

---

[2]"varying levels of noise and inhomogeneity" [6]
[3]Average over noise levels 1–9% and INU level 40%
[4]Average over noise level 0–9% and INU level 40%
[5]Average over noise levels 1–9% and INU levels 0% and 40%

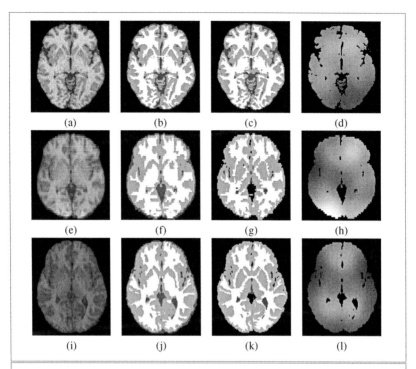

Figure 2.3: Axial slices of original images, the segmentation results, the ground-truth and the estimated INU field for one mono-spectral T1-weighted BrainWeb volume (5% noise, 20% INU) (a–d), one volume of the IBSR 20 Normal Subjects data set (e–h), and one volume of the IBSR 18 Subjects data set (i–l).

et al. [113] report results computed on data collections exclusively corrupted by an INU level of 40%.

Fig. 2.4 shows that INU, measured by the average COV, is reduced for all the spectral channels.

2.4.3 Quantitative Results on Mono-Spectral Simulated BrainWeb Data

As Table 2.5 shows, the results achieved for mono-spectral BrainWeb data are comparable to those of other state-of-the-art approaches to brain tissue classification [5, 93, 94, 6, 74, 4]. The results of Ashburner and Friston [4] are reported by Tsang et al. [107].

The results are better than those of van Leemput et al. [113] and the original HMRF-EM approach [129][6]. Awate et al. [5], van Leemput et al. [113], and Bazin and Pham [6] average over the same BrainWeb data sets as mentioned above for their experimental results. Again, comparability to the methods of Awate et al. [5] and van Leemput et al. [113] may be limited due to the fact that both are exclusively evaluated on BrainWeb data sets corrupted by an INU level of 40%. Scherrer et al. [93, 94] present average values in exactly the same manner as we do for our system. For Ashburner and Friston [4] and Zhang et al.'s HMRF-EM [129] the values are averaged over noise levels 1%, 3%, 5%, and 7% and INU level 20%. For Bricq et al. [13] the values are averaged over noise levels 0%, 1%, 3%, 5%, 7%, and 9% and INU level 20%, for Marroquin et al. [74] over noise levels 0%, 1%, 3%, 5%, 7%, and 9% and INU levels 0% and 20%. In accordance with Marroquin et al. [74] and Bricq et al. [13] we only observe a limited gain in segmentation accuracy when going from mono-spectral to multi-spectral data. This effect may be due to the fact that all the channels of the multi-spectral BrainWeb data set are generated from the same underlying phantom in a deterministic manner. Therefore the additional information provided about the phantom's true composition with respect to tissue types may be rather redundant than of any additive value. Fig. 2.3 gives a visual impression of the results obtained for mono-spectral input data. With regards to INU correction, it can be seen from Table 2.6(a) that the average COV is reduced.

2.4.4   Quantitative Results on Normal Subjects Mono-Spectral Scans

With regards to experimental comparison our method shows better results in terms of segmentation accuracy (Jaccard coefficient) than the methods of Akselrod-Ballin et al. [1] and Marroquin et al. [74] (see Table 2.7) for the IBSR 20 data set. In terms of the Dice coefficient DMC-EM reaches a higher accuracy for GM segmentation than the method of Ashburner and Friston [4][7] and the original HMRF-EM [129][8]. Table 2.6(b) shows that all the data sets were, on average, successfully corrected for INU.

As depicted in Figs. 2.5 and 2.6 DMC-EM constantly gives better results than pure HMRF-EM with zero-valued unary clique potentials and probabilistic atlas-based initialization. Except for a few cases it also gives better results than the HMRF-EM approach with probabilistic atlas-based unary clique potentials and probabilistic atlas-based initialization.

On the IBSR 18 data set our method performs comparably to other state-of-the-art approaches with regards to segmentation accuracy (see Table 2.8). However, one has to note here that the method of Akselrod-Ballin et al. [2] relies on stationary observation

---

[6]Reported by Tsang et al. [107]
[7]Reported by Tsang et al. [107]
[8]Reported by Tsang et al. [107]

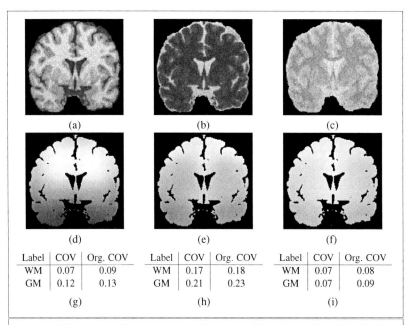

Label	COV	Org. COV
WM	0.07	0.09
GM	0.12	0.13

(g)

Label	COV	Org. COV
WM	0.17	0.18
GM	0.21	0.23

(h)

Label	COV	Org. COV
WM	0.07	0.08
GM	0.07	0.09

(i)

Figure 2.4: Coronary slices of original multi-spectral (T1-weighted, T2-weighted, and PD-weighted) BrainWeb images of 5% noise and 20% INU (a–c) and estimated INU fields (d–f). Average INU correction accuracy on multi-spectral BrainWeb data in terms of the COV before and after INU correction (g–i).

models that have been derived in a cross-validation setting from separate training volumes, which all origin from the same source of data. Their method might therefore be highly biased to uniform contrast characteristics present in the IBSR 18 data set and the results do not necessarily adequately reflect the performance of the method when applied to a larger variety of data sets in clinical practice. Even though the quantitative results of Awate et al. [5] are very impressive the visual impression of the segmentation results presented does not match with this observation as the coronal slices depicted there (p. 737, Figs. 5(b) and 5(c)) show obvious misclassifications especially at the outer bounds of the brain.

Figs. 2.7 and 2.8 show that the introduction of discriminative model dependent unary clique potentials and PBT initialization improves segmentation accuracy for the IBSR 18 data set. In comparison to the HMRF-EM approach with zero-valued unary clique potentials and probabilistic atlas-based initialization and to the HMRF-EM approach with probabilistic atlas-based unary clique potentials and probabilistic atlas-based initialization DMC-EM usually reaches a higher segmentation accuracy in terms of the Dice coefficient for GM and WM.

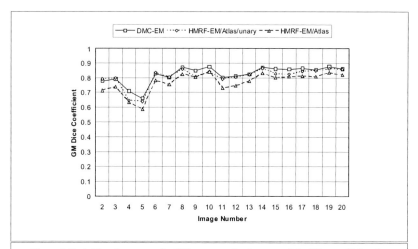

Figure 2.5: Achieved accuracy for GM segmentation in terms of the Dice coefficient for the IBSR 20 data set by the DMC-EM algorithm, the HMRF-EM algorithm with probabilistic atlas-based unary clique potentials and probabilistic atlas-based initialization, and the HMRF-EM algorithm with zero-valued unary clique potentials and probabilistic atlas-based initialization.

2.5 Discussion

Our newly proposed DMC-EM approach to fully automated 3-D Brain MRI tissue classi-fication and INU correction makes use of two different types of spatial priors: the first one, which contributes the unary clique potentials of the hidden Markov random field's Gibbs distribution, is derived from a strong discriminative model, in our case a PBT classifier, that has been built from annotated training data. It only makes use of features of reduced INU sensitivity and therefore prevents the model from over-fitting to scanner specific tissue contrast characteristics, which is experimentally validated by detailed evaluations on pub-licly available patient data sets from different sources and scanners. Usually, if the set of features is not carefully chosen, using supervised learning for MRI brain tissue classifica-tion ties a method to the exact acquisition protocol the classifier is trained for: for instance, Han et al. [54] introduced an intensity renormalization procedure into the method of Fischl et al. [37, 38]. As seen in our experiments an appropriate choice of features can help to cir-cumvent this dependency without the need for additional pre-processing. Our experimental setup did not allow specially adapted parameter settings for any of the data sets. All free parameters were kept fixed during experimentation. By not only including prior knowl-edge from an affinely preregistered probabilistic atlas our discriminative model is capable of producing more patient specific external fields. The second prior used, constituting the

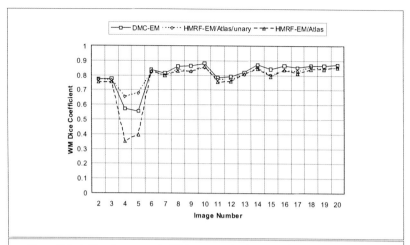

Figure 2.6: Achieved accuracy for WM segmentation in terms of the Dice coefficient for the IBSR 20 data set by the DMC-EM algorithm, the HMRF-EM algorithm with probabilistic atlas-based unary clique potentials and probabilistic atlas-based initialization, and the HMRF-EM algorithm with zero-valued unary clique potentials and probabilistic atlas-based initialization.

pair-wise clique potentials, is a smoothing prior that penalizes certain configurations in local neighborhoods depending on similarity of observed intensities, physical distance between image voxels, and estimated image noise. This makes the approach robust against different levels of noise, which is also shown by quantitative experimental evaluation.

From the theoretical point of view, in contrast to Zhang et al. [129], a consistent multi-spectral formulation of our DMC-EM framework both for brain tissue segmentation as well as for INU correction is presented. Accordingly, evaluation is carried out on mono- and multi-spectral patient data. On all the data sets our method achieves a segmentation accuracy that is either higher or comparable to the state-of-the-art even though progress in this highly investigated branch of research is difficult due to the well-established competitiveness of the methods available.

From visually inspecting our segmentation results we observe that our method seems to reveal weaknesses when it comes to deep GM structure segmentation. Even though the caudate nuclei and the putamen could be successfully segmented in all the images depicted in Fig. 2.3 the globus pallidus and the thalamus were misclassified in all the three image volumes. As both structures appear brighter than most of the other GM structures our observation model that models tissue classes as single Gaussian distributions seems too restrictive in this case. The problem may be solved by trying to model individual tissue classes, and not only the whole brain, by mixtures of Gaussians. In addition, more complex

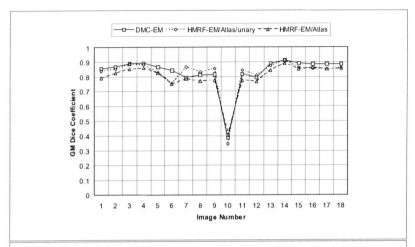

Figure 2.7: Achieved accuracy for GM segmentation in terms of the Dice coefficient for the IBSR 18 data set by the DMC-EM algorithm, the HMRF-EM algorithm with probabilistic atlas-based unary clique potentials and probabilistic atlas-based initialization, and the HMRF-EM algorithm with zero-valued unary clique potentials and probabilistic atlas-based initialization.

discriminative models could be considered that further decompose cervical GM into individual structures [126]. By doing so the dominance of the prior model over the observation model could be steered separately for individual anatomical entities.

It has to be mentioned also that particular high values for segmentation accuracy on the BrainWeb data sets (see Tables 2.4 and 2.5) do not necessarily mean a particular method is giving anatomically correct segmentation results. As depicted in Fig. 2.3(c) the associated ground-truth annotation suffers from obvious weaknesses in the area of the globus pallidus and the thalamus.

Concerning PVEs our method is conceptually predisposed to explicitly handle the effect that individual voxels may be composed of different tissue types due to the limited resolution of the acquisition devices. The inherent mixture model estimation of our algorithm provides an insight on how or to which degree different tissue types contribute to a certain voxel. However, we decided not to focus on handling PVEs and rather transform our results into hard classifications for evaluation purposes after algorithmic processing.

Similarly to, for instance, the method of Marroquin et al. [74] our method seems not to be of high accuracy with respect to CSF estimation. This may be caused by the fact that we consider the complete fluid filled space outside and inside the brain to be the CSF segment. It includes both the ventricular system as well as the subarachnoid space. Especially the segmentation of the latter may be subject to errors originating from imperfections of

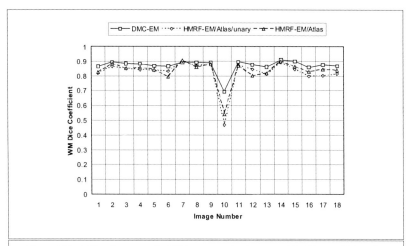

Figure 2.8: Achieved accuracy for WM segmentation in terms of the Dice coefficient for the IBSR 18 data set by the DMC-EM algorithm, the HMRF-EM algorithm with probabilistic atlas-based unary clique potentials and probabilistic atlas-based initialization, and the HMRF-EM algorithm with zero-valued unary clique potentials and probabilistic atlas-based initialization.

the initial skull stripping procedure. However, our method is carried out completely automatically without any user interaction. Results for CSF segmentation might be better if a "perfect" initial skull stripping was assumed.

With regards to INU correction our method suffers from the same limitations as the method of Wells et al. [119] does due to the fact that it forms the base of our approach. In a broader context, focusing on the method of Wells et al. [119] can be seen as an exemplary choice. Other more robust techniques that parametrically constrain estimated INU fields might in fact benefit in an equal manner if they were embedded in our modality-specific discriminative model-constrained HMRF-EM approach. DMC-EM is comparable fast when compared to other state-of-the-art approaches and it takes only a few minutes to process a data volume. The system presented in this chapter does not address sub-cortical segmentation but we will come back to this issue in Chapter 4. On the other hand, any generic state-of-the-art approach to organ segmentation will profit significantly from class-wise intensity standardized and INU corrected MRI input volumes.

2.6   Conclusions

We have presented an MRI modality-specific discriminative model-constrained HMRF-EM (DMC-EM) approach to brain tissue segmentation and INU correction in multi-spectral 3-D MRI. The major contribution of our work is a strong discriminative model obtained by a PBT classifier that is integrated into the framework by means of unary clique potentials in a mathematically sound manner. The discriminative model used is MRI modality specific as it only relies on features of reduced INU sensitivity taking into account the particularities of the MRI modality. As experimentally validated the choice of features prevents our method from being tied to a particular acquisition protocol at a specific site or scanner. Detailed quantitative evaluations on publicly available benchmarking databases demonstrate this increased robustness of our approach. At the same time the segmentation accuracy achieved is comparable to those of other state-of-the-art approaches to brain tissue classification in MRI data.

In the following chapter we will see how discriminative model-constrained MRF modeling and appropriate optimization techniques can be used to also address the problem of segmenting pathologic tissue types in multi-spectral 3-D MR images of the human brain—a common problem in neuroradiology that has not been considered in this chapter. Pathologic tissue is typically characterized by a high variability both in appearance as well as in shape and only occurs in patients suffering from a specific disease.

Method	Tissue Class	Dice Coeff.	Jaccard Coeff.
DMC-EM	WM	0.93 ± 0.03	0.87 ± 0.05
	GM	0.91 ± 0.05	0.83 ± 0.07
	CSF	0.76 ± 0.04	0.61 ± 0.05
Bricq et al. [13]	WM	0.95 ± 0.02	-
	GM	0.95 ± 0.03	-
	CSF	-	-
LOCUS-T [93]	WM	0.94	-
	GM	0.92	-
	CSF	0.80	-
FBM-T [94]	WM	0.94	-
	GM	0.92	-
	CSF	0.80	-
Bazin and Pham [6]	WM	0.94 ± 0.01	-
	GM	0.92 ± 0.02	-
	CSF	0.92 ± 0.01	-
Ashburner and Friston [4]	WM	-	-
	GM	0.92	-
	CSF	-	-
Marroquin et al. [74]	WM	0.93 ± 0.03	-
	GM	0.92 ± 0.03	-
	CSF	-	-
Awate et al. [5]	WM	0.95 ± 0.01	-
	GM	0.91 ± 0.01	-
	CSF	-	-
van Leemput et al. [113]	WM	0.90 ± 0.03	-
	GM	0.90 ± 0.02	-
	CSF	-	-
HMRF-EM [129]	WM	-	-
	GM	0.89	-
	CSF	-	-

Table 2.5: Average segmentation accuracy for mono-spectral (T1-weighted) simulated BrainWeb data of noise levels 1%, 3%, 5%, 7%, and 9%, and INUs of 20% and 40%. From left to right the columns contain the tissue class and the achieved average Dice and Jaccard coefficients.

Label	COV	Org. COV	Label	COV	Org. COV	Label	COV	Org. COV
WM	0.06	0.08	WM	0.08	0.09	WM	0.08	0.10
GM	0.12	0.13	GM	0.16	0.17	GM	0.16	0.18
(a)			(b)			(c)		

Table 2.6: Average INU correction accuracy in terms of the COV before and after INU correction for the mono-spectral BrainWeb data set (a), the IBSR 18 Subjects data set (b), and the IBSR 20 Normal Subjects Data set (c).

Method	Tissue Class	Dice Coeff.	Jaccard Coeff.
DMC-EM	WM	0.81 ± 0.09	0.69 ± 0.12
	GM	0.82 ± 0.06	0.71 ± 0.08
	CSF	0.83 ± 0.05	0.71 ± 0.07
Akselrod-Ballin et al. [1]	WM	-	0.67
	GM	-	0.68
	CSF	-	-
Marroquin et al. [74]	WM	-	0.68
	GM	-	0.66
	CSF	-	0.23
Ashburner and Friston [4]	WM	-	-
	GM	0.79	-
	CSF	-	-
HMRF-EM [129]	WM	-	-
	GM	0.76	-
	CSF	-	-

Table 2.7: Average segmentation accuracy for IBSR 20 with exclusion of data set No. 1 that has been used for training. From left to right the columns contain the tissue class and the achieved average Dice and Jaccard coefficients.

Method	Label	Dice Coeff.	Jaccard Coeff.
DMC-EM	WM	0.87 ± 0.05 (0.88 ± 0.01)	0.77 ± 0.06 (0.79 ± 0.02)
	GM	0.83 ± 0.12 (0.86 ± 0.04)	0.73 ± 0.13 (0.76 ± 0.06)
	CSF	0.76 ± 0.09 (0.77 ± 0.08)	0.62 ± 0.11 (0.63 ± 0.10)
Bazin and Pham [6]	WM	0.82 ± 0.04	-
	GM	0.88 ± 0.01	-
	CSF	-	-
Akselrod-Ballin et al. [2]	WM	0.87	-
	GM	0.86	-
	CSF	0.83	-
Awate et al. [5]	WM	0.89 ± 0.02	-
	GM	0.81 ± 0.04	-
	CSF	-	-
Bricq et al. [13]	WM	0.87 ± 0.02	-
	GM	0.80 ± 0.06	-
	CSF	-	-

Table 2.8: Average segmentation accuracy for IBSR 18. From left to right the columns contain the tissue label and the achieved average Dice and Jaccard coefficients for all the data sets and for data sets 1–9 and 11–18 with outlier data set 10 removed in brackets.

Chapter 3

Fully Automated Pediatric Brain Tumor Segmentation in 3-D MRI

In this chapter we present a fully automated approach to the segmentation of pediatric brain tumors in multi-spectral 3-D MRI images. It is a top-down segmentation approach based on an MRF model that combines PBTs and lower-level segmentation via graph cuts. The PBT algorithm provides a strong discriminative prior model that classifies tumor appearance while a spatial prior takes into account pair-wise voxel homogeneities in terms of classification labels and multi-spectral voxel intensities. The discriminative model relies not only on observed local intensities but also on surrounding context for detecting candidate regions for pathology. A mathematically sound formulation for integrating the two approaches into a unified statistical framework is given. The method is applied to the challenging task of detection and delineation of pediatric brain tumors. This segmentation task is characterized by a high non-uniformity of both pathology as well as surrounding non-pathologic brain tissue. Despite dealing with more complicated cases of *pediatric brain tumors* the results obtained in a quantitative evaluation are mostly better than those reported for current state-of-the-art approaches to 3-D MRI brain tumor segmentation in adult patients. The entire processing of one multi-spectral data set does not require any user interaction, and our method is about 20% faster than the fastest previously proposed method. It takes only 5 minutes to process one volume sequence including preprocessing. The main contributions of this chapter have been published in references [121] and [120]. Parts of the presented system have also been used in references [122] and [124].

3.1 Motivation

Detection and delineation of pathology, such as cancerous tissue, within multi-spectral brain MR images is an important problem in medical image analysis. For example, a precise and reliable segmentation of brain tumors present in the childlike brain is regarded

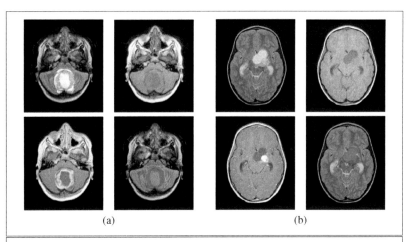

(a)   (b)

Figure 3.1: Two different cases of pediatric brain tumors exhibiting heterogeneous shape and appearance. Columns (a) and (b) show axial slices of the typically acquired pulse sequences (row-wise from left to right: T2-weighted, T1-weighted, and T1-weighted after contrast enhancement) and the expert annotated ground-truth overlaid to the T2-weighted pulse sequence.

critical when aiming for the automatic extraction of diagnostically relevant quantitative or more abstract findings. This may include the volume of the tumor or its relative location. Once these findings are obtained they can be used both for guiding CAD and therapy planning as well as for traditional decision making. However, the manual labeling of volumetric data is usually time consuming, which has the potential to delay clinical workflow, such that there is a need for fully automatic segmentation tools in this particular context. Furthermore, manual annotations may vary significantly among experts as a result of individual experience and interpretation.

As multi-spectral 3-D MRI is the method of choice for the examination of neurological pathology such as brain cancer in pediatric patients, automatic approaches first have to be capable of dealing with the characteristic artifacts of this imaging modality: Rician noise [80], PVEs [114], and intra-/inter-scan INUs [119, 60]. Second and more importantly, they have to be robust enough to handle the heterogeneous shape and appearance of pediatric brain tumors in different patients (see Fig. 3.1). In the case of pediatric brain tumors not only pathology underlies significant variation in shape and appearance but also the non-pathological "background", which is caused by ongoing myelination of WM during maturation [78]. This may cause WM to appear darker in pediatric T1-weighted MRI scans than in adult patient data sets.

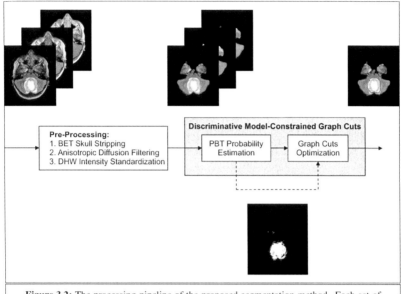

Figure 3.2: The processing pipeline of the proposed segmentation method. Each set of images schematically represents the input and/or output of individual processing steps.

In this chapter, we describe a fully automatic solution based on a novel top-down segmentation scheme that uses a statistical model of pathology appearance as a constraint for a subsequent optimization problem. The statistical model is provided by a machine learning technique that is able to work with high-dimensional feature vectors allowing to encode characteristic voxel contexts. The optimization problem itself is stated as a search for an MAP estimate of the most likely binary image segmentation, which permits efficient computation of a solution by means of a discrete max-flow/min-cut optimization procedure and is optimal in terms of Bayesian classification theory. The overall system block diagram, including preprocessing (brain extraction [100], smoothing, and MRI intensity standardization [29]) is depicted in Fig. 3.2.

3.2   Related Work

3.2.1   Preprocessing: MRI Inter-Scan Intensity Standardization

In general, MR images exhibit varying contrast characteristics even though they were acquired with an identical acquisition protocol but with a different scanner at a different site.
With regards to the distribution of intensities within images depicting the interior of the
human skull the associated histograms appear non-linearly deformed. These inter-scan
variations make image interpretation difficult as individual intensities lack a unique meaning regarding the underlying tissue type. This is especially true with regards to automatic
image post-processing like image segmentation that often heavily relies on observed intensity values when deciding on which tissue class a specific voxel of an image belongs
to. For this purpose several authors suggested approaches for MRI inter-scan intensity
standardization or normalization.

Nyúl et al. [81, 82] and Ge et al. [43] propose a two-step 1-D histogram matching
approach. In the first step, parameters (percentiles, modes, etc.) of the reference histogram
are derived from a set of reference images. In the second step, those parameters are used
to map the histogram of a newly acquired MR image onto the reference histogram by
matching specific landmark locations and linear interpolation.

Jäger and Hornegger [60] use a variational approach to register multivariate PDFs in
the form of multi-dimensional joint histograms for establishing intensity mappings for MRI
intensity standardization to multi-spectral template images.

In a similar manner, we try to find an intensity mapping between a reference image and
a newly acquired image by bringing the associated histograms into line with each other
during preprocessing. The method we use for histogram registration is based on dynamic
histogram warping (DHW) [29] from a technical perspective. The technique is strongly
related to dynamic time warping (DTW) [66], which is used for 1-D sequence comparison. However, we apply DHW to MRI volumes of the human brain in order to standardize
intensities and not for the purpose of achieving constant image brightness in 2-D images.
Later we will present a graph theoretic re-formulation of the original dynamic programming approach proposed by Cox and Hingorani [29]. For measuring similarity between
histograms we adapted it such that the Kullback-Leibler divergence [67] is minimized,
which is appropriate to measure PDF similarity.

3.2.2   MRI Brain Tumor Segmentation

Approaches in the field of MRI brain tumor segmentation rarely rely on pure data-driven
approaches, with Gibbs et al.'s method [47] being an early exception, due to the complexity in terms of tumor shape and appearance of the segmentation task. The vast majority

of methods make use of domain knowledge using different types of representation and combine it with low-level imaging techniques. Fletcher-Heath et al. [39] use unsupervised fuzzy clustering followed by 3-D connected components with an intermediate step incorporating knowledge about the usual distribution of CSF and location of the ventricular system. Ho et al. [57] have the evolution of a level set function guided by a tumor probability map that is generated by exploiting higher-level domain knowledge on how contrast enhancement in T1-weighted images affects tumor appearance. Corso et al. [26, 25] use the multi-level segmentation by weighted aggregation algorithm with tissue class-specific Gaussian mixture models for brain, tumor, and edema. Gering et al. [46] use trained parametric statistical models for intensity distributions of non-pathologic brain tissue to detect model outliers on the voxel level that are considered tumor voxels in a multi-layer MRF framework. In a similar manner Moon et al. [76, 75] and later Prastawa et al. [87, 88] detect outliers based on refined intensity distributions for healthy brain tissue initially derived from a registered probabilistic atlas, which introduces structural domain knowledge. Registration is also used in combination with voxel intensities in the adaptive template-moderated classification algorithm by Kaus et al. [64, 63]. More recent approaches try to enrich low-level segmentation techniques, like level set evolution [21] or hierarchical clustering [28], by using supervised machine learning on higher dimensional feature sets associated with each image voxel. These feature sets are capable of representing a more general variety of domain knowledge on different levels of abstraction. For instance, Zook and Iftekharuddin [132] analyze the fractal dimension of tumor area versus non-tumor area and show that this is a statistically significant indicator for tumor appearance. Based on this idea, Iftekharuddin et al. [58] use multi-resolution texture features generated by a combination of fractal Brownian motion and wavelet multi-resolution analysis together with self-organizing maps. In a similar manner we make use of the recently proposed technique of PBTs [108] in combination with 2-D [83, 115] and 3-D Haar-like features [111] for supervised learning, which has proven its robustness and its capability for efficient training and classification in numerous applications [110, 18]. Both types of features are closely related to 3-D Haar-like features of reduced INU sensitivity, which are explained in Chapter 2 in more detail. The probability estimates provided by PBT are then used to constrain the highly efficient computation of minimum cuts [11] for image segmentation based on an MRF prior model. It takes into account both coherence of classification labels as well as multi-spectral intensity similarities within voxel neighborhoods.

3.2.3 Image Segmentation Using Max-Flow/Min-Cut Computation

In this chapter, we give an integrated formulation for combining PBT classification and computation of minimum cuts. Opposed to other methods [26, 28, 25, 21] there is no involvement of a time consuming bias field correction step in data preprocessing in our approach. In the case of Corso et al. [26, 28, 25] this seems to be done by FAST [129], which relies on an HMRF-EM segmentation approach. In the presence of abnormal tissue types this requires the determination of the number of different intensity regions expected within each scan. Furthermore, this inherent low-level segmentation might bias the final segmentation result. In contrast we build discriminative models, that is, PBTs, whose generalization capabilities are strong enough to implicitly handle those intra-patient intensity non-uniformities. Moreover, we apply our method to the more complicated task of segmenting pediatric brain tumors.

3.3 Preprocessing: DHW for Non-Parametric MRI Inter-Scan Intensity Standardization

The problem of body region-specific mono-spectral MRI inter-scan intensity standardization can be stated as follows: Let $\mathcal{V} = \{1, \ldots, V\}$, $V \in \mathbb{N}$, and $\mathcal{W} = \{1, \ldots, W\}$, $W \in \mathbb{N}$, bet sets of indices to image voxels, and $\mathcal{I} = \{0, \ldots, 2^b - 1\}$ be a set of gray scale intensities with a given bit-depth $b \in \mathbb{N}$. For two 1-D discrete PDFs $p_f : \mathcal{I} \to (0, 1]$ and $p_g : \mathcal{I} \to (0, 1]$, which are two histograms of equidistant bin size, of two MRI volumes $\boldsymbol{f} = (f_i)_{i \in \mathcal{V}}$, $f_i \in \mathcal{I}$, (acquired image) and $\boldsymbol{g} = (g_i)_{i \in \mathcal{W}}$, $g_i \in \mathcal{I}$, (reference image) of the same body region acquired with an identical pulse sequence find a mapping

$$u : \mathcal{I} \to \mathcal{I} \tag{3.1}$$

that makes $p_{\boldsymbol{u}(\boldsymbol{f})}$, $\boldsymbol{u}(\boldsymbol{f}) = (u(f_i))_{i \in \mathcal{V}}$, "most" similar to the reference histogram p_g. For simplicity let $p = p_f$ and $q = p_g$, and $p_\nu = p_f(\nu)$ and $q_\nu = p_g(\nu)$ the corresponding values for any $\nu \in \mathcal{I}$ in the following. Accordingly, let P_ν and Q_ν be the values of the associated (cumulative) probability distributions P and Q.

Let $G = (V, E, \alpha, \beta)$ be a directed graph with vertices

$$V = \{(\nu, \mu) | \nu, \mu \in \mathcal{I}\} \tag{3.2}$$

and edges

$$\begin{aligned} E = \ & \{((\nu - 1, \mu - 1), (\nu, \mu)) \,|\, 1 \leq \nu \leq 2^b - 1, 1 \leq \mu \leq 2^b - 1\} \cup \\ & \{((\nu - \kappa, \mu - 1), (\nu, \mu)) \,|\, 1 \leq \kappa \leq M, \kappa \leq \nu \leq 2^b - 1, 1 \leq \mu \leq 2^b - 1\} \cup \\ & \{((\nu - 1, \mu - \lambda), (\nu, \mu)) \,|\, 1 \leq \nu \leq 2^b - 1, 1 \leq \lambda \leq N, \lambda \leq \mu \leq 2^b - 1\}. \end{aligned} \tag{3.3}$$

Here $\alpha(e)$ and $\beta(e)$ denote the vertices where edge e starts and ends, respectively. The weight of an edge, that is, the distance or dissimilarity between two adjacent graph vertices,

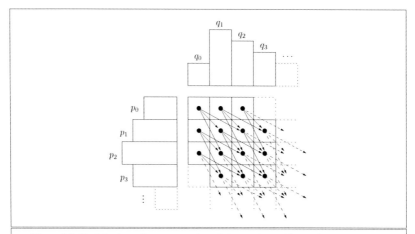

Figure 3.3: Partial schematic representation of the graph considered ($M = 2, N = 2$) and its relation to the initial discrete PDFs $p = p_f$ and $q = p_g$. The vertices $(\nu, \mu) \in V$ of G are depicted as dots aligned in a quadratic scheme of maximum size $2^b - 1 \times 2^b - 1$. The edges E are depicted as arrows.

can then be defined as a mapping $d : E \to \mathbb{R}$ representing the non-negative summands of any with respect the number of bins monotonic additive bin-by-bin histogram dissimilarity measure. The dissimilarity measure is implicitly applied to deformed versions of p and q where for an edge $e = ((\nu - \kappa, \mu - 1), (\nu, \mu))$ an amount of κ successive bins of p are contracted. In an equal manner an edge $e = ((\nu - 1, \mu - \lambda), (\nu, \mu))$ represents the contraction of λ successive bins of q, which corresponds to the uniform expansion of one bin of p. This vice-versa relation is of particular interest as we want to deform p non-linearly to match q, which can be achieved as follows: due to the specific structure of G a shortest path $w = (e_1, \ldots, e_t)$ along vertices $(v_1, \ldots, v_{t+1})$ from $(0, 0)$ to $(2^b - 1, 2^b - 1)$ can be computed efficiently via dynamic programming. This gives, on the one hand, the minimum distance $D(p', q') = \sum_{i=1}^{t} d(e_i)$ of deformed histograms p' and q' achievable at the given constraints M and N, and, on the other hand, the associated mapping that makes p most similar to q. The corresponding assignment for u is then

$$u(\nu) = \pi_2^{(2)}(v_{i+1}) \text{ for } \pi_1^{(2)}(v_i) < \nu \leq \pi_1^{(2)}(v_{i+1}), i \in \{1, \ldots, t\}. \quad (3.4)$$

Here $\pi_2^{(2)} : \mathcal{I} \times \mathcal{I} \to \mathcal{I}$ with $\pi_2^{(2)}(\nu, \mu) = \mu$ for all $\nu, \mu \in \mathcal{I}$ denotes the projection on the second component of a two-dimensional vertex. Analogously, $\pi_1^{(2)}$ is the projection on the first component of a two-dimensional vertex.

Note that the parameters M and N serve as smoothness constraints as they steer allowed deformation relative to the major diagonal of the underlying graph scheme (see Fig. 3.3).

Possible dissimilarity measures (see Rubner et al. [92] for details) involve the simplest Minkowski-form distance $D_{L_1}(p,q) = \sum_\nu |p_\nu - q_\nu|$ where the edge weight would be

$$d_{L_1}((\nu - \kappa, \mu - \lambda), (\nu, \mu)) = |(P_\nu - P_{\nu-\kappa}) - (Q_\mu - Q_{\mu-\lambda})|. \tag{3.5}$$

It is also possible to use the discrete Kullback-Leibler divergence in its symmetrical form $D_{KL}(p,q) = \sum_\nu (p_\nu - q_\nu) \cdot \log(p_\nu/q_\nu)$ with according edge weight

$$d_{KL}((\nu - \kappa, \mu - \lambda), (\nu, \mu)) = ((P_\nu - P_{\nu-\kappa}) - (Q_\mu - Q_{\mu-\lambda})) \cdot \log\left(\frac{P_\nu - P_{\nu-\kappa}}{Q_\mu - Q_{\mu-\lambda}}\right). \tag{3.6}$$

Both distances are additive, i.e., separable, and monotonic with respect to the number of bins of the two input histograms considered. Monotonicity is ensured due to the fact that the summands involved are strictly non-negative. Separability and simultaneous monotonicity state the precondition for making distance measures applicable in the context of dynamic programming. Other dissimilarity measures like, for instance, the earth mover's distance (EMD) [92], may better match the intuition of dissimilarity between different PDFs. However, their computation is usually more complex and their separable and monotonic reformulation may be non-trivial or even impossible.

Fig. 3.4 shows exemplary results for several volumetric brain MR images. For all the experiments we restricted intensity standardization to brain soft tissue only in order to prevent background voxels from dominating the standardization process and therefore achieving sub-optimal results. Skull stripping was achieved by preprocessing the data sets with FSL BET [100]. Likewise, the background can also be excluded by simple thresholding methods.

3.4 Segmentation Method

Our segmentation method relies on the integrated formulation of an objective function that is subject to optimization via the efficient graph cuts algorithm [11]. In the following we derive this objective function from the general MAP framework for image segmentation.

3.4.1 Posterior Mode Image Segmentation

In general, the problem of segmenting an image can be stated as the search for an MAP estimate of the most likely class labels given appropriate prior and observation models in terms of PDFs. Let $\mathcal{S} = \{1, 2, \ldots, N\}$, $N \in \mathbb{N}$, be a set of indices to image voxels. At

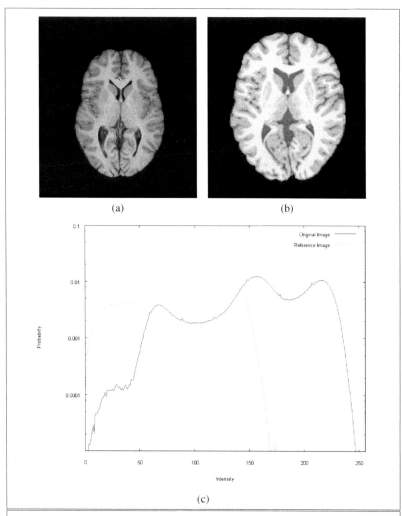

Figure 3.4: Axial slice of a reference volumes (a) and axial slice of an original volume (b) and associated histograms with 256 bins (c). All images displayed at identical intensity window.

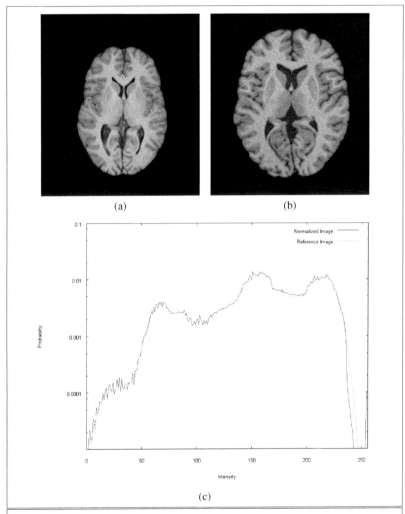

Figure 3.5: Axial slice of a reference volumes (a) and axial slice of a normalized volume
(b) and associated histograms with 256 bins (c). All images displayed at
identical intensity window.

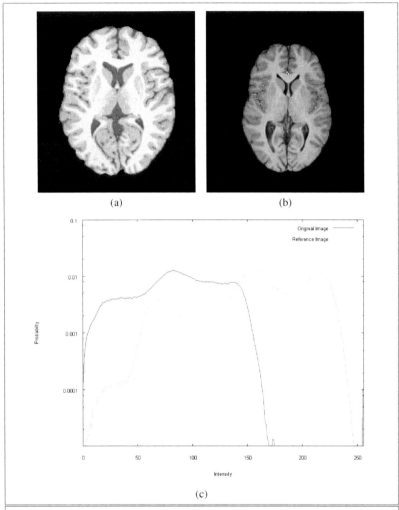

Figure 3.6: Axial slice of a reference volumes (a) and axial slice of an original volume (b) and associated histograms with 256 bins (c). All images displayed at identical intensity window.

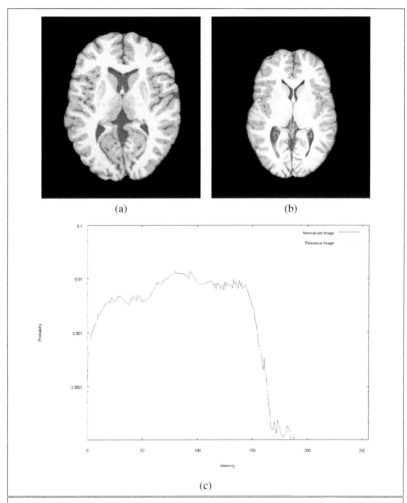

(a)   (b)

(c)

Figure 3.7: Axial slice of a reference volumes (a) and axial slice of a normalized volume
(b) and associated histograms with 256 bins (c). All images displayed at
identical intensity window.

each index $s \in \mathcal{S}$ there are two random variables: $y_s \in \mathcal{Y} = \{+1, -1\}$ and $\boldsymbol{x}_s \in \mathcal{X} = \mathbb{R}^M$, $M \in \mathbb{N}$. The former, y_s, denotes the unobservable binary segmentation of voxel s into fore- and background, whereas the latter, $\boldsymbol{x}_s$, states the observable vector of multi-spectral intensities that are assumed to be causally linked to the underlying class labels $y \in \mathcal{Y}$ by a unified observation model defined by a PDF $p(\boldsymbol{x}|y)$ for $\boldsymbol{x} \in \mathcal{X}$. The emergence of the class labels themselves is described by a prior model $p(y)$. The segmentation task at hand can now be stated as the search for an MAP estimate

$$\boldsymbol{Y}^* = \arg\max_{\boldsymbol{Y}} p(\boldsymbol{Y}|\boldsymbol{X}) \tag{3.7}$$

where $p(\boldsymbol{Y}|\boldsymbol{X})$ is the joint posterior probability over the image domain $\mathcal{S}$ with $\boldsymbol{Y} = (y_s)_{s \in \mathcal{S}}$ and $\boldsymbol{X} = (\boldsymbol{x}_s)_{s \in \mathcal{S}}$. Using Bayes' rule and the independence of $p(\boldsymbol{X})$ from $\boldsymbol{Y}$, we have:

$$\boldsymbol{Y}^* = \arg\max_{\boldsymbol{Y}} \ln p(\boldsymbol{X}|\boldsymbol{Y}) + \ln p(\boldsymbol{Y}). \tag{3.8}$$

To concretize this optimization problem a region-specific probability term and an appropriate prior need to be identified.

3.4.2 Histogram-Based Observation Model

We assume the multi-spectral observations to be independently and identically distributed (i.i.d.), that is, $p(\boldsymbol{X}|\boldsymbol{Y}) = \prod_{s \in \mathcal{S}} p(\boldsymbol{x}_s|y_s)$. The PDFs for that are estimated during segmentation via histograms by understanding an initial PBT voxel classification as intermediate segmentation that is close to the final result.

3.4.3 Discriminative Model-Constrained MRF Prior Model

For the prior distribution we assume an MRF prior model

$$p(\boldsymbol{Y}) \propto \exp(-U(\boldsymbol{Y}; \frac{1}{\lambda})) \tag{3.9}$$

formulated, according to the Hammersley-Clifford Theorem, as a Gibbs distribution with energy function

$$U(\boldsymbol{Y}; \frac{1}{\lambda}) = \sum_{s \in \mathcal{S}} \left(V_s(y_s) + \frac{1}{\lambda} \sum_{t \in \mathcal{N}_s} V_{st}(y_s, y_t) \right) \tag{3.10}$$

where $\frac{1}{\lambda}$ with $\lambda \in (0, +\infty)$ controls the relative influence of the spatial prior, i.e., the pairwise clique potentials, over the external influences, i.e., the unary clique potentials. The set $\mathcal{N}_s$ describes the neighborhood of voxel s. As done in Chapter 2 we ignore higher-ordered clique potentials.

The unary clique potentials $V_s(y_s)$ are provided by a PBT classifier. As described in Appendix A the PBT provides an approximation $\tilde{p}(y_s|\boldsymbol{z}_s)$ of the true posterior probability $p(y_s|\boldsymbol{z}_s)$ at its root node for feature vectors $\boldsymbol{z}_s$ associated with individual voxels s. Here $y_s \in \{-1, +1\}$ denotes the classification outcome, that is, background or foreground. Thus, we have

$$V_s(y_s) = \ln \tilde{p}(y_s|\boldsymbol{z}_s). \tag{3.11}$$

For our first experiment, the feature vectors $\boldsymbol{z}_s$ used for PBT classification consist of individual multi-spectral intensities, inter-channel intensity gradients, and 2-D Haar-like features [83, 115] computed on an intra-axial 2-D context surrounding the voxel of interest. The Haar-like features are derived from a subset of the extended set of Haar-like feature prototypes [70] and are represented only implicitly in memory by (rotated) integral images. This allows fast re-computation of the features with respect to a given voxel when they are actually assessed. As we intend to capture a discriminative representation of the full 2-D context, and not only of local edge characteristics at the central voxel, 2-D Haar-like feature values are computed according to the given prototypes on every valid origin and scale within the chosen voxel context.

For our second experiment, the feature vectors $\boldsymbol{z}_s$ used for PBT probability estimation consist of individual multi-spectral intensities and multi-spectral 3-D Haar-like features [108] computed on a 3-D context surrounding the voxel of interest. The Haar-like features are derived from a set of 3-D Haar-like feature prototypes centered at the voxel of interest and are held implicitly in memory by means of integral volumes. Equally to the 2-D case, the features are re-computed on-the-fly when they are actually assessed.

Similar to what is done in Chapter 2 the pair-wise interaction potentials are

$$V_{st}(y_s, y_t) = \exp\left(-\frac{1}{2}\sum_{l=1}^{L}\frac{(x_{s_l} - x_{t_l})^2}{\sigma_l^2}\right) \cdot \frac{\delta(y_s, y_t)}{\text{dist}(s, t)} \tag{3.12}$$

where vectors $\boldsymbol{x}_s = (x_{s_1}, \ldots, x_{s_L})^T$ and $\boldsymbol{x}_t = (x_{t_1}, \ldots, x_{t_L})$ denote the observed intensities at voxels s and t taken from $L \in \mathbb{N}$ aligned input pulse sequences.

3.4.4 Discriminative Model-Constrained Graph Cuts Segmentation

With the equality

$$
\begin{aligned}
\boldsymbol{Y}^* &= \arg\max_{\boldsymbol{Y}} \sum_{s\in\mathcal{S}} \ln p(\boldsymbol{x}_s|y_s) + \sum_{s\in\mathcal{S}} V_s(y_s) - \frac{1}{\lambda}\sum_{s\in\mathcal{S}}\sum_{t\in\mathcal{N}_s} V_{st}(y_s, y_t) \\
&= \arg\min_{\boldsymbol{Y}} \left(\sum_{s\in\mathcal{S}} -\lambda \cdot (\ln p(\boldsymbol{x}_s|y_s) + V_s(y_s))\right) + \sum_{s\in\mathcal{S}}\sum_{t\in\mathcal{N}_s} V_{st}(y_s, y_t) \quad (3.13)
\end{aligned}
$$

the initial maximization problem can be transformed into a minimization problem that is in a suitable form for optimization by the graph cuts algorithm [11]. Note that the reciprocal of the regularization parameter in (3.10) can equivalently be used to weight the influence of the external influences in combination with the observation model over the prior model.

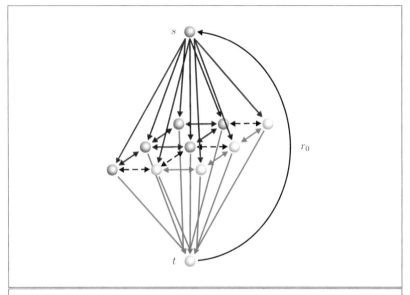

Figure 3.8: Example of a max-flow/min-cut problem instance with its associated extended graph. Vertex s denotes the source node and vertex t the sink node. The flow value on edge $r_0 = (t, s)$ is about to be optimized. The edges of a possible cut separating the green from the red vertices are displayed as dashed arrows.

The graph cuts algorithm [11] originates from the family of max-flow/min-cut algorithms within combinatorial optimization theory. They can be used [11, 52] to minimize energies of the form

$$E(\boldsymbol{Y}) = \sum_{s \in \mathcal{S}} D_s(y_s) + \sum_{s \in \mathcal{S}} \sum_{t \in \mathcal{N}_s} V_{st}(y_s, y_t). \qquad (3.14)$$

In our case the data penalty function is given by

$$D_s(y_s) = -\lambda \cdot (\ln p(\boldsymbol{x}_s | y_s) + V_s(y_s)). \qquad (3.15)$$

whereas the interaction potentials V_{st} remain unchanged.

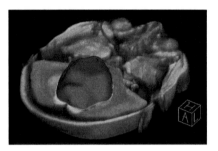

Figure 3.9: The rendered result for patient No. 1 overlaid on the T2-weighted pulse sequence. Due to the coarse axial resolution the extracted surface has been smoothed [106] before rendering.

Let the graph $M = (V, E)$ with vertices $V = \{ v_s \mid s \in \mathcal{S} \}$ and edges $E = \{ (v_s, v_t) \mid s \in \mathcal{S}, t \in \mathcal{N}_s \}$ represent the associated MRF described before. The objective of any max-flow/min-cut computation is to find a maximum flow in the extended directed weighted graph $G = (V', E', c)$ where the set of vertices $V' = V \cup \{ s, t \}$ is extended by two terminal nodes—the source node s and the sink node t. The edges of the graph are $E' = E \cup \{ (s, v) \mid v \in V \} \cup \{ (v, t) \mid v \in V \} \cup \{ (t, s) \}$, and the function $c : E' \to \mathbb{R} \cup \{ +\infty \}$ denotes the edge capacities. A flow is a function $\beta : E' \to \mathbb{R}$ with $\sum_{(v_i, v_j) \in V: v_j = v} \beta(v_i, v_j) = \sum_{(v_i, v_j) \in V: v_i = v} \beta(v_i, v_j)$ for all $v \in V$. It is admissible with respect to c if and only if $0 \leq \beta(r) \leq c(r)$ for all $r \in E'$. The maximum flow β^* searched for reaches the highest possible flow value on edge (t, s) among all admissible flows, that is, $\beta^* = \arg\max_\beta \beta(t, s)$. In accordance with Equation (3.13) the capacities are

$$c(v_i, v_j) = \begin{cases} V_{ij}(y_i, y_j) & \text{if } v_i \neq s \text{ and } v_j \neq t, \\ D_j(y_j = -1) & \text{if } v_i = s, \\ D_i(y_i = +1) & \text{if } v_j = t. \end{cases} \tag{3.16}$$

According to the theorem of Ford and Fulkerson the problem of finding a maximum flow is equivalent to the problem of finding a minimum cut, which is a partition $C^* = S^* \cup T^*$, $S^* \cap T^* = \emptyset$ with $s \in S^*$ and $t \in T^*$, whose cost $\sum_{(v_i, v_j): v_i \in S, v_j \in T} c(v_i, v_j)$ is minimal among all possible cuts. Note that a minimum cost cut equivalently defines a globally optimal binary labeling, that is to say, a segmentation, of the graph nodes. Fig. 3.8 shows an exemplary max-flow/min-cut problem with its associated graph.

Boykov and Kolmogorov [11] identified two categories of combinatorial optimization algorithms for this kind of problem: 1) Goldberg-Tarjan style "push-relabel" algorithms and 2) Ford-Fulkerson style "augmenting paths" algorithms. Either type has polynomial time complexity.

In "push-relabel" algorithms [48] there are active nodes having excess flow, i.e., inflow that has not yet been explained by an appropriate outflow to a neighboring node and its connections to the sink node. During optimization for every node a heuristic is kept that gives a low bound estimate on the cost to reach the sink starting from that point along non-saturated edges. In the course of computing the maximum flow the excess flows are stepwise propagated to nodes being closer to the sink node with regards to the estimated distance. This so-called push operation is typically applied to active nodes with the highest estimated distance to the sink node or based on a FIFO selection strategy. Alternatively, the heuristic value of a node can be updated in a relabel operation. Both operations are applied as long as the accompanying preconditions are met.

In "augmenting paths" algorithms [40, 36, 32] the overall flow in the graph is successively increased along augmenting paths in the so-called residual graph, which stores information about the remaining available capacities in the network. This is repeated as long as there are such augmenting paths. In the beginning the edge capacities in the residual graph are equal to those in the original graph and there is not any flow from the source to the sink. In each iteration it is searched for a path [40] or shortest path [36, 32], in the sense of the amount of edges involved, from source to sink in the residual graph. If such a path is found the algorithm augments the overall flow in the network by increasing it along the involved edges such that at least one of the edges in the path is completely saturated. Accordingly, the remaining capacities along the augmenting path are decreased by exactly the same amount in the residual graph. Saturated edges are not considered any further.

Formally, the residual graph associated with G and an admissible flow β is defined as $G_\beta = (V, E'_\beta)$ where $E'_\beta = \{ e^1 | e \in E' \setminus \{ (t, s) \}, \beta(e) < c(e) \} \cup \{ e^{-1} | e \in E' \setminus \{ (t, s) \}, \beta(e) > 0 \}$ and $\pi_1^{(2)}(e^1) = \pi_1^{(2)}(e)$ and $\pi_2^{(2)}(e^1) = \pi_2^{(2)}(e)$, and $\pi_1^{(2)}(e^{-1}) = \pi_2^{(2)}(e)$ and $\pi_2^{(2)}(e^{-1}) = \pi_1^{(2)}(e)$ for all $e \in E'$. An augmenting path is a path $p = (e_1^{\delta_1}, \ldots, e_k^{\delta_k})$, $k \in \mathbb{N}$, in G_β with the following properties: (1) $\pi_1^{(2)}(e_1^{\delta_1}) = s$, $e_1 \neq (t, s)$, and $\pi_2^{(2)}(e_k^{\delta_k}) = t$, $e_k \neq (t, s)$, (2) $\forall_{i:\delta_i=1}\beta(e_i) < c(e_i)$, and (3) $\forall_{i:\delta_i=-1}\beta(e_i) > 0$.

While the Edmonds-Karp [36] or Dinic [32] algorithm use breadth-first search to completely rebuild the tree of shortest paths in G_β from time to time, Boykov and Kolmogorov [11] integrated strategies to decrease computation time used for this expensive operation to a minimum (see Algorithm 2). In step 1 of their algorithm two search trees are used, one from the source and the other one from the sink. They are reused to find an augmenting path in every iteration, and never completely rebuilt. In step 2 the current flow is increased along the found augmenting path. Accordingly, saturated edges are removed from the residual graph. Thus, the search trees may be split into forests and some of their nodes may become orphans, that is, the connections to their parent nodes are no longer part of G_β. In the adoption stage (step 3) the forests are tried to be reconnected to form two search trees again. We refer to the original work of Boykov and Kolmogorov [11] for details on the three steps involved.

Algorithm 2: Graph cuts algorithm

Input: extended directed weighted graph G, an admissible flow β
Output: minimum cut $C^* = S^* \cup T^*$ and a maximum flow β^*
begin

    // Initialize search trees
    $S \to \{s\}, T \to \{t\}$;

    // Enter main loop
    while *true* **do**
        1. Grow S or T to find an augmenting path p from s to t;
        if p *empty* **then**
          | break;
        end
        2. Augment β on p;
        3. Adopt orphans;
    end

    // Return minimum cut and maximum flow
    $S^* = S, T^* = T, \beta^* = \beta$;
    return S^*, T^*, β^*;
end

The augmenting paths found in step 1 of Algorithm 2 are not necessarily shortest augmenting paths. Therefore, the worst case time complexities of the Edmonds-Karp algorithm ($\mathcal{O}(|V||E'|^2)$) and Dinic algorithm ($\mathcal{O}(|V|^2|E'|)$) relying on this fact are no longer valid. However, the cost of the maximum flow $\beta^*(t, s)$ after rescaling capacities to integer values is an upper bound on the number of augmentations needed for the algorithm. Thus, the worst case complexity is $\mathcal{O}(|V|^2|E'| \cdot \beta^*(t, s))$. Though no longer guaranteeing optimal worst case runtime complexity the approach of Boykov and Kolmogorov has proven to significantly outperform other standard algorithms in various experiments. [11]

3.4.5 Summary

In total, our approach to pediatric brain tumor segmentation can be summarized as shown in Algorithm 3. We will refer to our algorithm as the discriminative model-constrained graph cuts algorithm (DMC-GC).

3.5 Validation

3.5.1 Experimental Setup

For quantitative evaluation of the proposed method there were six multi-spectral expert annotated data sets of pediatric patients aged from 1 year and 5 months to 15 years and

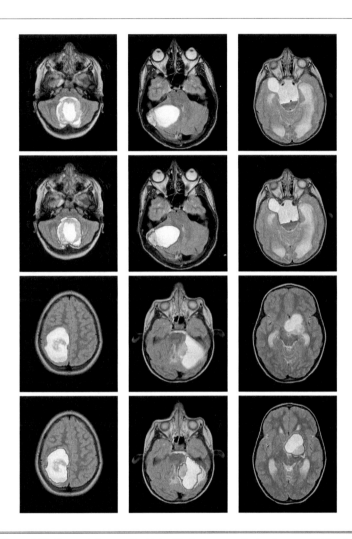

Figure 3.10: Segmentation results obtained by leave-one-patient-out cross validation for
a system using 2-D Haar-like features. The odd rows show selected slices of
the T2-weighted pulse sequences of the six available patient data sets. The
even rows show the associated segmentation results (red) and the ground-
truth segmentation (green) overlaid on the T2-weighted pulse sequence.

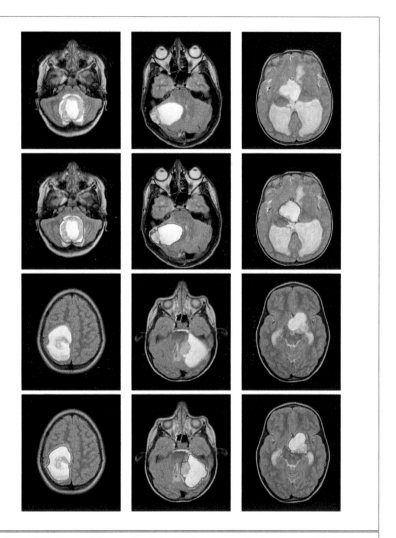

Figure 3.11: Segmentation results obtained by leave-one-patient-out cross validation for a system using 3-D Haar-like features. The odd rows show selected slices of the T2-weighted pulse sequences of the six available patient data sets. The even rows show the associated segmentation results (red) and the ground-truth segmentation (green) overlaid on the T2-weighted pulse sequence.

Algorithm 3: DMC-GC algorithm

Input: (multi-spectral) MRI volume X
Output: binary segmentation Y
begin

  PBT probability estimation for unary clique potentials (see Equation (3.11));
  Fore-/background observation model generation based on threshold $\bar{p}(+1|z_s) \geq 0.5$;
  Computation of binary segmentation Y through optimizing Equation (3.13) via graph cuts
  algorithm (see Algorithm 2);
end

---

10 months available—among them four pilocytic astrocytomas, one pilomyxoid astrocytoma, and one anaplastic astroblastoma. Each scan consists of three 3-D images acquired at different pulse sequences (T2-weighted, T1-weighted, and T1-weighted after contrast enhancement). The resolution is $512 \times 512 \times 20$ with a voxel spacing of $0.45 \times 0.45 \times 6.0$ mm^3. Where necessary due to patient movement during image acquisition the pulse sequences were co-aligned by means of the MedINRIA affine registration tool (www-sop.inria.fr/ asclepios/software/MedINRIA). As mentioned above, all the sequences were preprocessed by the following pipeline: skull stripping by the BET [100], gradient anisotropic diffusion filtering (www.itk.org), and MRI inter-scan intensity standardization by DHW [29]. Note that all of the preprocessing steps involved, including co-alignment, can be performed fully automatically without any user interaction. We refer to Appendix B for details on the mask-based segmentation accuracy measures used in Tables 3.1 and 3.2.

The PBT voxel classifiers built were restricted to a maximum depth of 10 with 10 weak classifiers per tree node. The graph cuts optimization, using Vladimir Kolmogorov's publicly available implementation [11], is carried out on the original image resolution with $\mathcal{N}_s$ defined to be a standard 6-neighborhood on the 3-D image lattice. The standard deviation $(\sigma_1, \ldots, \sigma_L)$ for the interaction potentials in (3.12) was estimated offline as "camera noise" within manually delineated homogeneous regions throughout the patient volumes.

It takes about 1–2 minutes to process one of the multi-spectral MRI volumes in a non-optimized C++ implementation of our segmentation method on a Fujitsu Siemens Computers notebook equipped with an Intel Pentium M 2.0 GHz processor and 2 GB of memory. With the same hardware as above training one classifier takes about 4 hours. Preprocessing the images takes about 3 minutes so a total amount of 5 minutes is needed for processing one patient data set. In terms of total processing time our method is therefore faster than the method of Corso et al. [28], which is claimed to be fastest among current approaches to fully automatic MRI brain tumor segmentation.

3.5.2 Quantitative Results Using 2-D Haar-Like Features

For our first experiment with 2-D Haar-like features we considered a voxel context of size 11×11 on volumes down-sampled to a voxel spacing of $2.0 \times 2.0 \times 6.0$ mm^3. A leave-one-

Data set	Dice	Jaccard	Pearson
1	0.93	0.87	0.93
2	0.93	0.87	0.93
3	0.90	0.81	0.90
4	0.96	0.92	0.96
5	0.63	0.46	0.67
6	0.85	0.73	0.85
Average	0.86	0.78	0.87

Table 3.1: Performance indices obtained by leave-one-patient-out cross validation fo a system using 2-D Haar-like features for all of the examined data sets. From left to right the columns contain the achieved Dice coefficient, Jaccard coefficient, and Pearson correlation coefficient.

out cross validation on the patient data sets and their accompanying PBT models yielded best average segmentation scores in terms of the Jaccard coefficient for $\lambda \in [0.1, 0.5]$ such that finally $\lambda = 0.2$ was chosen for computing the results depicted in Fig. 3.10. In order to remove small regions of false positive voxels only the largest connected component of the graph cuts result is considered to be the final segmentation. With Jaccard coefficients of 0.78 ± 0.17 the segmentation results are better than those published by Cobzas et al. (0.60) [21] and, except for one case, in a similar range as those of Corso et al., (0.85) [26] and (0.86) [28], who all work with adult patient data sets and partly on four pulse sequences [28]. However, comparability of results is limited because of different characteristics between the data sets used by the mentioned scientists, for example, pediatric patients versus adult patients, additional usage of more expressive pulse sequences, presence of necrotic tissue within the tumors, restriction to a certain histological type of tumor, etc.

3.5.3 Quantitative Results Using 3-D Haar-Like Features

In our second experiment with 3-D Haar-like features we considered a voxel context of size $25 \times 25 \times 8$ likewise on volumes down-sampled to a voxel spacing of $2.0 \times 2.0 \times 6.0$ mm^3. A leave-one-patient-out cross validation on the data sets and their accompanying PBT models yielded best average segmentation scores in terms of the Jaccard coefficient for $\lambda \in [0.03, 0.06]$ such that finally $\lambda = 0.05$ was chosen for computing the results depicted in Figs. 3.9 and 3.11. With an average Jaccard coefficient of 0.81 ± 0.05 (see Table 3.2) the segmentation results are better than those published by Cobzas et al. (0.60) [21] and Wels et al. (0.78) [121] and in a similar range as those of Corso et al., (0.85) [26] and

Data set	Dice	Jaccard	Pearson
1	0.93	0.87	0.93
2	0.92	0.85	0.92
3	0.87	0.78	0.88
4	0.89	0.81	0.90
5	0.89	0.80	0.89
6	0.85	0.73	0.85
Average	0.89	0.81	0.90

Table 3.2: Performance indices obtained by leave-one-patient-out cross validation for a system using 3-D Haar-like features for all of the examined data sets. From left to right the columns contain the achieved Dice coefficient, Jaccard coefficient, and Pearson correlation coefficient.

(0.86) [28], where some methods [21, 28, 26] work with adult patient data sets and partly on four pulse sequences [28].

3.6 Discussion

The most limiting aspect for the method presented arises from the variety in tumor appearance. Whereas non-pathologic tissue types usually share a rather regular appearance pathologic tissue types such as pediatric brain tumors do not: pathologic vascularization may or may not be involved. There can be multiple cysts within the pathologic complex, which are typically filled with CSF complicating dissociation of the ventricular system. The presence of the tumor may have led to the formation of an edema surrounding pathology. Finally, parts of the tumor may already have become necrotic contributing another possible manifestation of tumor tissue. An appropriate appearance model would have to be capable of anticipating any of these possible tissue types, which was only possible for our system through building more general models based on a larger amount of training data better capturing variation of tumor appearance. In contrast, the standard composition of the healthy brain follows certain regularities, which is a fact our system, as presented in this chapter, does not take into consideration more explicitly. However, we could show by experimentation that our discriminative model is able to capture the heterogeneous appearance of pediatric brain tumors and non-pathologic background when appropriate training data is given.

Similarly as with tumor appearance, expert users may use different annotation protocols depending on the purpose of their computer-aided radiological decision making. These differences in protocols may cause difficulties for fully automatic brain tumor segmentation.

For an initial characterization of the disease at hand the whole pathologic complex is of interest and tumor surrounding edema can give a clue in explaining certain neuropathological symptoms. For image-guided surgery or radiotherapy edema and the cystic portion of the tumor are merely of secondary interest. Further delineation of the pathologic complex into different parts, for example, cystic portion, necrotic portion, and solid tumor tissue, may be of additional value.

With regards to preprocessing, while inter-scan intensity non-uniformities are addressed by means of DHW, our approach lacks an appropriate way to deal with intra-scan intensity non-uniformities. As seen in the previous chapter many of the methods, including the one presented there, assume the brain not to be invaded by new tissue types, which will necessarily be the case if it comes to a brain tumor. The presence of non-foreseen tissue types may also affect the distribution of intensities, and the assumption that the histogram of the acquired image is a deformed version of the histogram of the standardization template may no longer hold. In such cases DHW, or any other histogram registration technique, is likely to give suboptimal results.

In the approach presented in this chapter, the discriminative probability estimates are generated for every voxel regardless whether its classification is critical, that is, it is close to the tumor boundary, or not. Typically, one is more interested in an accurate delineation along the boundaries of the pathologic tissue rather than in the pure classification into fore- and background voxels. Evaluating every voxel can become a costly operation as soon as the data considered has a higher axial resolution. In this case, however, the 3-D context will be much more distinct, which may allow to build stronger discriminative models based on 3-D Haar-like features.

Even though solutions to those limiting factors could not be addressed in the scope of this chapter and for the introduced system, the used methodology of discriminative model-constrained graph cuts optimization for pediatric brain tumor segmentation in 3-D MRI shows how discriminative and generative modeling can be combined. The improved mathematical representation given clearly identifies the unary clique potentials of the MRF prior model as the key concept for imposing external constraints from a strong discriminative model on the segmentation process. The segmentation problem itself is modeled as a Bayesian classification problem, which by its nature at first involves generative modeling. Previously, we intended to use the discriminative model directly as observation model. [121]

Furthermore, the application of a proven optimal algorithm for optimizing the derived objective function representing the segmentation problem prevents the method from being attracted by local minima—a problem generally faced by gradient descend methods whose derivation rely only on a necessary but not sufficient condition for optimality of the solution. However, any method, optimal or approximative, for optimizing MRF posterior probabilities in the form of Equation (3.13), for example, ICM [9] as used in Chapter 2, can replace the chosen optimization strategy from a practical point of view. The generic nature of the discriminative model-constrained graph cuts approach presented in this chapter may also allow the approach to be applied in domains other than pediatric brain tumor detection and segmentation. As shown by our experiments multi-spectral input data can easily be brought in the process of discriminative model generation by pulse sequence specific (Haar-like) features. In fact, it can be taken advantage of any "clues" for classification at the level of individual voxels.

We did not try and use any shape model like it will be done in Chapter 4 for deep gray matter structure detection and segmentation, which would indeed be inappropriate for brain tumor segmentation due to the high irregularity of not only tumor appearance but also tumor shape.

3.7 Conclusions

The contribution of this chapter is threefold: we presented a graph theoretic reformulation of DHW and applied it to the preprocessing problem at hand, that is, MRI inter-scan intensity standardization. Then, starting from the well-known MAP framework for image segmentation we derived a constrained minimization problem suitable for max-flow/min-cut optimization via the graph cuts algorithm that incorporates an observation model provided by a discriminative PBT classifier into the process of segmentation. Furthermore, we successfully applied the method to the difficult problem of fully automatic pediatric brain tumor segmentation in multi-spectral 3-D MRI. The experimental results obtained are mostly better than those recently published for fully automatic brain tumor segmentation in adult patients.

In the following chapter we will come back to the problem of segmenting the usual, non-pathologic brain anatomy in 3-D MR images of the human brain. We will focus in particular on the segmentation of (sub-)cortical GM structures. Chapter 4 naturally extends Chapter 2 from a conceptual point of view as we are now interested in a finer decomposition of the brain's anatomy while we only addressed the common tissue types, which are GM, WM, and CSF, beforehand.

Chapter 4

3-D MRI Brain Structure Segmentation

In this chapter, we present a novel method for the automatic detection and segmentation of (sub-)cortical gray matter structures in 3-D MR images of the human brain. Essentially, the method is a top-down segmentation approach based on the recently introduced concept of marginal space learning (MSL). We show that MSL naturally decomposes the parameter space of anatomy shapes along decreasing levels of geometrical abstraction into subspaces of increasing dimensionality by exploiting parameter invariance. At each level of abstraction, that is, in each subspace, we build strong discriminative models from annotated training data, and use these models to narrow the range of possible solutions until a final shape can be inferred. Contextual information is introduced into the system by representing candidate shape parameters with high-dimensional vectors of 3-D generalized Haar features and steerable features derived from the observed volume intensities. Unlike most approaches in the literature, we allow for inter-patient intensity non-uniformities, typical in MRI examinations, and handle them with a fast intensity standardization strategy based on DHW as it is also done in Chapter 3. Likewise, for the sake of an increased generalization capability of the final system, we do not assume the scans to be spatially normalized or skull stripped. Our system allows us to detect and segment 8 (sub-)cortical gray matter structures in T1-weighted 3-D MRI brain scans from a variety of different scanners in 13.9 seconds, on average. In order to ensure comparability of the achieved results and to validate robustness, we evaluate our method on two publicly available gold standard databases consisting of several T1-weighted 3-D brain MRI scans from different scanners and sites. The proposed method achieves an accuracy better than most state-of-the-art approaches using standardized distance and overlap metrics. The main contributions of this chapter have been published in reference [126]. A predecessor system has been described in reference [123].

69

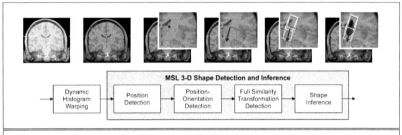

Figure 4.1: The processing pipeline of the proposed 3-D shape detection and inference method. Each image (detection and delineation of the left caudate) schematically represents the input and/or output of individual processing steps.

4.1   Motivation

Currently, many scientific questions in neurology, like the revelation of mechanisms affecting generative or degenerative processes in brain development, require quantitative volumetric analysis of (sub-)cortical gray matter structures in large populations of patients and healthy controls. For instance, atrophy in the presence of Alzheimer's disease considerably affects morphology of the hippocampus. In addition, 3-D segmentation of various deep gray matter structures facilitates image-based surgical planning, therapy monitoring, and the generation of patient-specific geometrical models from imaging data for further processing. As a result of unclear boundaries, shape complexity, and different anatomical definitions, precise manual delineation is usually time consuming and user dependent. Moreover, typical artifacts present in MRI (Rician noise [80], PVEs [114], and intra-/inter-scan INUs [119, 60]) challenge the consistency of manual delineations. Therefore, a system for the automatic detection and segmentation of (sub-)cortical gray matter structures not only has the potential to increase segmentation consistency, but also has the capability of facilitating large-scale neuromorphological studies.

We propose a fully automatic method for the detection and delineation of the following eight (sub-)cortical gray matter structures: the left and right caudate nucleus, hippocampus, globus pallidus, and putamen. Our method consists of two major steps: 1) following an idea of Jäger and Hornegger [60], we standardize the observed MRI intensities by non-rigidly aligning their histogram to a template histogram by means of DHW [29] (see Chapter 3 for details); and 2) for each (sub-)cortical structure of interest we detect and infer its position, orientation, scale, and shape in an extended MSL framework [130, 131], which explicitly integrates shape inference into the overall MSL formulation. Fig. 4.1 depicts the complete processing pipeline of the proposed method.

4.2 Related Work

Recent methods [77, 109, 27] for (sub-)cortical gray matter structure segementation in 3-D MRI make use of machine learning in a similar manner as we do, but follow a bottom up approach ascending from the lowest level of abstraction, that is, the level of individual voxels, to the level of complete anatomical entities. Note that the methods mentioned above require the input volumes to be spatially normalized before the segmentation workflow can take place, which is a step that is not present in our approach. In references [77, 109, 27] a partly manually initialized nine parameter (translation, orientation, and anisotropic scaling) registration is part of the systems presented. Also, the feature pools for discriminative model generation are usually enriched by features explicitly encoding normalized location. [77, 109] In accordance with this observation, Tu et al. [109] and Corso et al. [27] only evaluate on spatially normalized data sets from one type of MRI scanner that are not publicly available. Nevertheless, Morra et al. [77] report state-of-the-art results on data sets that were not subject to spatial normalization.

Alignment of a probabilistic atlas by means of an twelve parameter affine registration also plays an important role in other approaches [94, 2]. While in reference [94] quantitative evaluation is only carried out on simulated data, the method of Akselrod-Ballin et al. [2] is trained and evaluated on only one publicly available dataset that has been subject to a specific preprocessing including intensity standardization. By generating observation or discriminative models based on intensity values without explicitly allowing for inter-scan intensity variations [77, 109, 27, 2], the models are at the risk of being over-adapted to specific contrast-characteristics of the data at hand. Morra et al. [77] repudiate this conceptual objection by achieving a high segmentation accuracy on data sets whose intensities were not standardized. In turn, Pohl et al. [85] take into account intensity inhomogeneities in their statistical framework for combined atlas registration and segmentation but do not provide details on whether the data sets used for evaluation contain varying intensity characteristics, that is to say, come from different scanners and sites. Bazin and Pham [6], presenting an atlas-based segmentation that combines topological and statistical atlases, evaluate their method on a larger variety of publicly available data sets, amongst them the ones we use for validation of our system.

From a technological point of view our approach is related to the following methods: Zheng et al. [130, 131] were the first to introduce MSL and apply it to automatic segmentation and geometrical modeling of the four heart chambers from 3-D cardiac CT volumes. Further developments and derivations of the methodology are used for polyp detection and segmentation in 3-D CT colonography [73], liver segmentation in 3-D abdominal CT [71], and semantic indexing of fetal anatomies from 3-D ultrasound [17, 19]. It is also applied for tracking the left heart ventricle in 4-D ultrasound sequences [127] and the aortic valve in 4-D CT sequences [59].

4.3   Method

4.3.1   Combined 3-D Shape Detection and Shape Inference

For combined 3-D rigid anatomy detection and shape inference we use a method based on the concept of MSL [130, 131]. We estimate the structure of interest's center $c = (c_1, c_2, c_3) \in \mathbb{R}^3$, orientation $R \in \mathcal{SO}(3)$, scale $s = (s_1, s_2, s_3)^T \in \{ s \in \mathbb{R}^3 \mid s_i > 0, i = 1, 2, 3 \}$, and shape $x = (x_1, y_1, z_1, \ldots, x_n, y_n, z_n)^T \in \mathbb{R}^{3n}$. The shape consists of canonically sampled 3-D points $x_i = (x_i, y_i, z_i)^T$, $i \in \{ 1, \ldots, n \}$, on the surface of an object to be segmented. Note that R is relative to c, s is relative to c and R, and x is relative to c, R, and s. Let $\mathcal{V} = \{ 1, 2, \ldots, N \}$, $N \in \mathbb{N}$, be a set of indices to image voxels, $Y = (y_v)_{v \in \mathcal{V}}$, $y_v \in \{ -1, 1 \}$, a binary segmentation of the image voxels into object and non-object voxels, and f be a function with $Y = f(I, \Theta)$ that provides a binary segmentation of volume I using segmentation parameters $\Theta = (c, R, s, x)$. Let $Z = (z_\Theta)$ be a family of high-dimensional feature vectors extracted from a given input volume $I = (i_v)_{v \in \mathcal{V}}$ and associated with different discretized configurations of Θ. In our context Z includes voxel-wise context encoding 3-D generalized Haar-like features [111] (see Chapter 2) to characterize possible object centers and steerable features [130, 131] that are capable of representing hypothetical orientations and optionally scaling relative to a given object center or shape surface point. These features were chosen for our method because of their fast computation and effective representation as demonstrated in references [130, 131].

We search for the optimal parameter vector

$$\Theta^* = \arg\max_{\Theta} p(y = 1 | \Theta, I, M^{(\Theta)}) = \arg\max_{\Theta} p(y = 1 | Z, M^{(\Theta)}) \qquad (4.1)$$

maximizing the posterior probability of the presence, that is, $y = 1$, of a sought anatomy given the discriminative model $M^{(\Theta)}$ and the features Z extracted from the input volume I using a certain set of values for the parameters Θ.

Let $\pi^{(c)}(Z)$, $\pi^{(c,R)}(Z)$, $\pi^{(c,R,s)}(Z)$, $\pi^{(c,R,s,x)}(Z)$ denote the vectors of components of Z associated with individual groups of elements (c), (c, R), (c, R, s), and (c, R, s, x) of the parameter vector Θ. The MSL method avoids exhaustively searching the high-dimensional parameter space spanned by all the possible Θ by exploiting the fact that ideally for any discriminative model for center detection with parameters $M^{(c)}$ working on a restricted amount of possible features

$$c^* = \arg\max_{c} p(y = 1 | \pi^{(c)}(Z), M^{(c)}) \qquad (4.2)$$

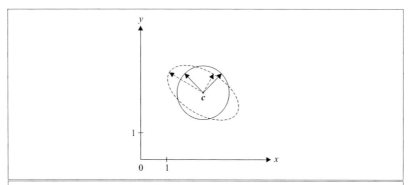

Figure 4.2: Invariance of $c \in \mathbb{R}^2$ under relative reorientation, relative anisotropic rescaling and relative shape positioning.

holds, as the object center is invariant under relative reorientation, relative rescaling, and relative shape positioning. Similarly, we have

$$R^* = \arg\max_{R} p(y = 1|\pi^{(c^*,R)}(Z), M^{(c,R)}) \tag{4.3}$$

for combined position-orientation detection with model parameters $M^{(c,R)}$ where only features $\pi^{(c^*,R)}(Z)$ with $c = c^*$ are considered. This is due to the fact that position and orientation are invariant under relative rescaling and relative shape positioning. Equations (4.2) and (4.3) are illustrated for the 2-D case where $c \in \mathbb{R}^2$ and $R \in \mathcal{SO}(2)$ in Figs. 4.2 and 4.3. Analogous considerations yield

$$s^* = \arg\max_{s} p(y = 1|\pi^{(c^*,R^*,s)}(Z), M^{(c,R,s)}) \tag{4.4}$$

for the object's scaling, and

$$x^* = \arg\max_{x} p(y = 1|\pi^{(c^*,R^*,s^*,x)}(Z), M^{(c,R,s,x,y,z)}, M^{(c,R,s,x)}) \tag{4.5}$$

for the object's shape where $M^{(c,R,s,x,y,z)}$ are the parameters of a local shape model with respect to individual surface points $(x, y, z)^T$ and parameters $M^{(c,R,s,x)}$ represent a global shape model.

Equations (4.2)–(4.5) naturally set up a chain of discriminative models exploiting search space parameter invariance for combined 3-D shape detection and shape inference. It allows us to apply different discriminative models descending along geometrical abstraction as, in our framework, the object center c alone is the most abstract and the complete set of parameters Θ is the least abstract shape representation. Therefore, MSL establishes

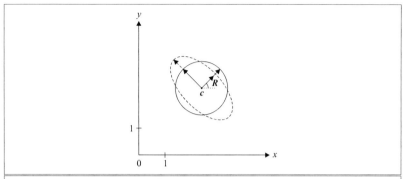

Figure 4.3: Invariance of $c \in \mathbb{R}^2$ and $R \in \mathcal{SO}(2)$ under relative anisotropic rescaling and relative shape positioning.

a hierarchical decomposition of the search space along decreasing levels of geometrical abstraction with increasing dimensionality of the considered parameter subspace.

4.3.2   3-D Shape Detection: Similarity Transformation Estimation

Let $\mathcal{Z}$ be the set of annotated image volumes in their transformed feature representation as mentioned above. We will refer to $\mathcal{Z}$ as the training data. In order to find the first parts of the optimal parameter vector Θ^* describing a nine parameter similarity transformation, that is, $c^* \in \mathbb{R}^3$, $R^* \in \mathcal{SO}(3)$, and $s^* \in \{\, s \in \mathbb{R}^3 \,|\, s_i > 0, i = 1, 2, 3 \,\}$, we have to learn discriminative models $p(y = 1|\pi^{(c)}(Z))$, $p(y = 1|\pi^{(c^*, R)}(Z))$, and $p(y = 1|\pi^{(c^*, R^*, s)}(Z))$. Following the concept of MSL [130, 131] we generate a set of positive and negative training examples $\mathcal{C} = \{\, (\pi^{(c)}(Z), y) \,|\, Z \in \mathcal{Z} \,\}$ to train a PBT model [108] for position detection. The feature vectors $\pi^{(c)}(Z)$ consist of 3-D generalized Haar-like features [111] encoding the voxel context of candidate object centers based on observed intensity values. Decreasing the level of geometric abstraction we analogously train a PBT model for combined position-orientation detection based on an extended set of training examples $\mathcal{G} = \{\, (\pi^{(c, R)}(Z), y) \,|\, Z \in \mathcal{Z} \,\}$ where $\pi^{(c, R)}(Z)$, associated with (c, R) and an image volume, is made of 3-D steerable features [130, 131]. They allow varying 3-D orientations and 3-D scalings to be encoded in terms of aligned and scaled intensity sampling patterns. Various 2-D steerable features encoding different 2-D orientations and 2-D scalings with respect to a 2-D point of interest are depicted in Fig. 4.4. In accordance with this scheme, steerable features are also used to finally train a PBT for full nine parameter similarity transformation detection based on $\mathcal{S} = \{\, (\pi^{(c, R, s)}(Z), y) \,|\, Z \in \mathcal{Z} \,\}$ where $\pi^{(c, R, s)}(Z)$ is derived from (c, R, s) and the associated image volume.

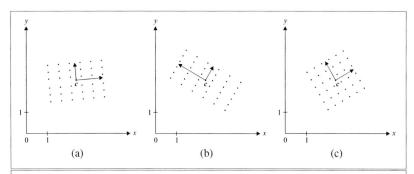

Figure 4.4: 2-D steerable features encoding different orientations and scalings with respect to a 2-D point of interest $c \in \mathbb{R}^2$ (a–c).

4.3.3 3-D Shape Inference under Global Shape Constraints

For the final object shape we further decompose

$$\pi^{(c,R,s,x)}(Z) = \left(\pi^{(c,R,s,x_i,y_i,z_i)}(Z) \right)_{i=1,\dots,n}$$

where $\pi^{(c,R,s,x_i,y_i,z_i)}(Z)$ are the features associated with an image volume and individual relatively aligned candidate points (c, R, s, x_i, y_i, z_i) for the surface of the object of interest. In order to apply discriminative modeling we assume the $(x_i, y_i, z_i)^T$ and correspondingly $\pi^{(c,R,s,x_i,y_i,z_i)}(Z)$ to be i.i.d. and approximate

$$
\begin{aligned}
x^* &= \arg\max_x p(y = 1 | \pi^{(c^*,R^*,s^*,x)}(Z), M^{(c,R,s,x,y,z)}, M^{(c,R,s,x)}) \\
&\approx \arg\max_x \left[\prod_{i=1}^{n} p(y_i = 1 | \pi^{(c^*,R^*,s^*,x_i,y_i,z_i)}(Z), M^{(c,R,s,x,y,z)}) \right] \\
&\quad \cdot p(x | c^*, R^*, s^*, M^{(c,R,s,x)})
\end{aligned}
\tag{4.6}
$$

in an iterative manner. The term $p(y_i = 1 | \pi^{(c,R,s,x_i,y_i,z_i)}(Z))$ describes the probability that the relatively aligned point (c, R, s, x_i, y_i, z_i) is part of the shape to be inferred, that is, lies on its surface, and $p(x | c^*, R^*, s^*, M^{(c,R,s,x)})$ is a global shape model [24]. We estimate $p(y = 1 | \pi^{(c,R,s,x,y,z)}(Z))$ with a PBT model [108] using steerable features [130, 131] trained on $\mathcal{X} = \{ (\pi^{(c,R,s,x,y,z)}(Z), y) | Z \in \mathcal{Z} \}$. An iterative approach to minimize Equation (4.6) is suitable as, in practice, $x = (x_1, y_1, z_1, \dots, x_n, y_n, z_n)^T \in \mathbb{R}^{3n}$ only varies around the mean shape positioned relatively to the (c^*, R^*, s^*) detected before at time $t = 0$ and the previous most likely anatomy shape in each iteration $t = 1, \dots, T$.

4.3.4 Global Shape Model

Active Shape Models

The concept of active shape models (ASM) allows for prior shape information during segmentation. They have been proposed by Cootes et al. [23, 24]. In the following we explain them in accordance with the presentation in reference [103]. The shapes are represented by clouds of points, which are either manually or automatically placed at certain characteristic locations within the class of images to be processed. Once these sets of labeled point features, or landmarks, are established for each image they are linearly aligned to each other in order to remove translation, rotation, and scaling as far as possible. This is done using generalized Procrustes analysis (GPA) [51], which is described in detail in Appendix C. After GPA all the shapes are transformed to a common coordinate system—the model space of the ASM. The remaining variability can be described as a prior model by means of a point distribution model (PDM).

Point Distribution Models

Let $y_1, y_2, \ldots, y_N$, $N \in \mathbb{N}^+$, be aligned shapes in the model space with sequences of $n \in \mathbb{N}^+$ points $y_i = (x_{i_1}, y_{i_1}, z_{i_1}, \ldots, x_{i_n}, y_{i_n}, z_{i_n})^T \in \mathbb{R}^{3n}$ for $i \in \{1, \ldots, N\}$. The mean shape $\bar{y}$ is given by

$$\bar{y} = \frac{1}{N} \sum_{i=1}^{N} y_i. \tag{4.7}$$

The associated covariance matrix can be computed by

$$\bar{S} = \frac{1}{N-1} \sum_{i=1}^{N} (y_i - \bar{y})(y_i - \bar{y})^T. \tag{4.8}$$

Let

$$D = \frac{1}{\sqrt{N-1}} (y_1 - \bar{y}, \ldots, y_N - \bar{y}) \in \mathbb{R}^{3n \times N} \tag{4.9}$$

be the whitened design matrix of the shape population. The covariance matrix can now be rewritten to

$$\bar{S} = DD^T. \tag{4.10}$$

Principal component analysis (PCA) by means of singular value decomposition (SVD) of $D = U\Sigma V^T$ with $U = (u_{ij})_{i=1,\ldots,3n, j=1,\ldots,3n} \in \mathbb{R}^{3n \times 3n}$, $\Sigma = (\sigma_{ij})_{i=1,\ldots,3n, j=1,\ldots,N} \in \mathbb{R}^{3n \times N}$, and $V = (v_{ij})_{i=1,\ldots,N, j=1,\ldots,N} \in \mathbb{R}^{N \times N}$ yields the $3n$ eigenvectors $u_i = (u_{1i}, \ldots, u_{3ni})^T$, $i \in \{1, \ldots, 3n\}$, associated with eigenvalues $\sigma_{11}^2 \geq \ldots \geq \sigma_{3n3n}^2$ of $\bar{S}$ on the main diagonal of $\Sigma\Sigma^T$. Using only $m \in \{1, \ldots, 3n\}$ eigenvectors any shape y in the training set can be approximated in shape space by

$$\boldsymbol{y} \approx \bar{\boldsymbol{y}} + \boldsymbol{P}\boldsymbol{b} \tag{4.11}$$

where $\boldsymbol{P} = (\boldsymbol{u}_1, \ldots, \boldsymbol{u}_m)$ is the matrix of the m selected eigenvectors, and $\boldsymbol{b} = (b_1, \ldots, b_m)^T$ are the shape parameters. The value of m is chosen such that a sufficently large portion of the total variance

$$\tau = \sum_{k=1}^{N} \tau_k, \tag{4.12}$$

$\tau_k = \sigma_{kk}^2$, in the training data can be explained by the model. For instance, Zheng et al. [131] choose m such that $\tau \leq 0.98$. By varying the values of $\boldsymbol{b}$ different shapes can be generated. Assuming a multivariate Gaussian distribution the probability for one particular shape $\boldsymbol{y}$ is given by

$$p(\boldsymbol{y}) = \left(\frac{1}{\prod_{i=1}^{m} 2\pi\sigma_{ii}^2} \right)^{\frac{1}{2}} \exp\left(-\frac{1}{2} \sum_{i=1}^{m} \left(\frac{b_i}{\sigma_{ii}} \right)^2 \right). \tag{4.13}$$

So, restricting the shape parameters by m is equal to setting the contribution of eigenvectors $\boldsymbol{u}_{m+1}, \ldots, \boldsymbol{u}_N$ in the shape space representation of the current shape to zero. Therefore, for any given shape in shape space representation the overall shape probability is increased by this projection onto an m-dimensional subspace of the shape space.

During model fitting a current shape $\boldsymbol{x}$ in real space is deformed by a displacement vector $\Delta\boldsymbol{x} = (\Delta x_1, \Delta y_1, \Delta z_1, \ldots, \Delta x_n, \Delta y_n, \Delta z_n)^T$. In our case the displacement is generated by sampling candidate surface points along the normal of each shape point of $\boldsymbol{x}$ in a certain range. In order to apply shape constraints on the new shape $\boldsymbol{x} + \Delta\boldsymbol{x}$ it has to be transformed to the model space of the ASM such that it can be represented via the mean shape and a linear combination of eigenvectors similar to Equation (4.11). By means of full ordinary Procrustes analysis (OPA) [34] (see Appendix C) we obtain

$$(\hat{s}, \hat{\boldsymbol{R}}, \hat{\boldsymbol{t}}) = \arg\min_{s, \boldsymbol{R}, \boldsymbol{t}} \|\bar{\boldsymbol{y}} - M(s, \boldsymbol{R}, \boldsymbol{t})[\boldsymbol{x} + \Delta\boldsymbol{x}]\|^2 \tag{4.14}$$

where $\|\boldsymbol{y}\| = (\sum_{i=1}^{n} x_i^2 + y_i^2 + z_i^2)^{\frac{1}{2}}$ is the Euclidean norm. The operator $M(s, \boldsymbol{R}, \boldsymbol{t})[\boldsymbol{x}]$ applies the similarity transformation associated with scaling factor s, orientation $\boldsymbol{R}$, and translation $\boldsymbol{t}$ to all points of $\boldsymbol{x}$. We are now able to transform the deformed shape into the model space of the ASM yielding $M(\hat{s}, \hat{\boldsymbol{R}}, \hat{\boldsymbol{t}})[\boldsymbol{x}]$. Thus, the variation of the shape that cannot be explained by the mean shape but, instead, needs to be explained by the shape parameters is

$$\boldsymbol{P}\boldsymbol{b} = M(\hat{s}, \hat{\boldsymbol{R}}, \hat{\boldsymbol{t}})[\boldsymbol{x}] - \bar{\boldsymbol{y}} \tag{4.15}$$

as we want $\bar{y} + Pb \approx M(\hat{s}, \hat{R}, \hat{t})[x]$. The update of the shape parameters is then given by

$$b = P^T (M(\hat{s}, \hat{R}, \hat{t})[x] - \bar{y}) \tag{4.16}$$

since $P^T = P^{-1}$. By transforming back to real space we get the new shape instance

$$x' = M^{-1}(\hat{s}, \hat{R}, \hat{t})[\bar{y} + Pb]. \tag{4.17}$$

Model Generation

Even though our approach relies on triangular meshes as the appropriate representation of ground-truth annotations all the annotations we used for model generation are only available as mask annotations. That is, they are represented as volume data sets of exactly the same size as the original volumes with all the voxels labeled with respect to the (sub-)cortical structure they belong to. In order to transform these to mesh representations we first use the marching cubes algorithm [72] to construct densely sampled triangular meshes. Then, for establishing topologically meaningful point correspondences between individual surface points $(x_{i_k}, y_{i_k}, z_{i_k})^T$ and $(x_{j_k}, y_{j_k}, z_{j_k})^T$, $k \in \{1, \ldots, n\}$, of different shapes x_i and x_j by construction we canonically resample the resulting shapes in the following manner: 1) For more spherical structures like the putamen or the globus pallidus we use a spherical coordinate system to parameterize the organ surface similarly to what is done by Ling et al. [71] and Seifert et al. [95]. Specifically, we define a function $S(\gamma, \phi) \in \mathbb{R}^3$, $\gamma \in [0, \pi]$, $\phi \in [0, 2\pi)$ that canonically maps spherical coordinates γ and ϕ to the surface of a given shape with respect to its center c and local coordinate system R. The parameters c and R are chosen to be the input mesh's center of gravity and the eigenvectors of a PCA applied to the mesh's surface points, respectively. In practice, the ranges of the zenith angle γ and the azimuth angle ϕ are sampled uniformly and for any discrete configuration the function value $S(\gamma, \phi)$ is chosen to be the point where the ray

$$g = c + \lambda \begin{pmatrix} \cos\phi \sin\gamma \\ \sin\phi \sin\gamma \\ \cos\gamma \end{pmatrix}, \lambda \geq 0, \tag{4.18}$$

intersects with the surface of the input shape; 2) for more tubular structures like the caudate nucleus or the hippocampus we also make use of the marching cubes algorithm to generate initial meshes from mask annotations. We define $T(t, \phi) \in \mathbb{R}^3$, $t \in [0, 1]$, $\phi \in [0, 2\pi)$ to parametrical resample mesh surface points with respect to an approximated compact

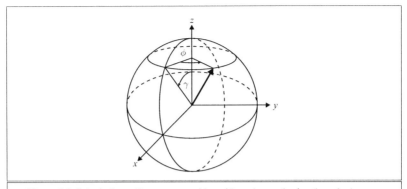

Figure 4.5: Spherical coordinate system with zenith angle γ and azimuth angle ϕ.

centerline $c(t) \in \mathbb{R}^3, t \in [0, 1]$, and the local coordinate system R. For any discrete t and discrete ϕ the function value $T(t, \phi)$ is set to be the point where the ray

$$g = c(t) + \lambda \begin{pmatrix} \cos\phi \\ \sin\phi \\ 0 \end{pmatrix}, \lambda \geq 0, \qquad (4.19)$$

perpendicular to $\nabla c(t)$ intersects with the surface of the input shape.

After shape generation all the shapes that are about to be used for model generation are registered to each other and transformed into a common coordinate system by means of GPA as mentioned above.

For each structure the parameters (s, R, t) for rigid shape detection are estimated based on the resampled ground-truth shape annotations x. A local orthonormal coordinate system is computed with orientation R and origin t, which is the center of gravity, via PCA. The anisotropic scaling factors s are determined according to the maximum extensions of the shape in predefined directions along the local coordinate axes.

4.3.5 Meta-Structure Detection

As pointed out by Zheng et al. [130] using MSL for rigid detection of each anatomy independently is not by any means optimal. Intuitively, the positions of (sub-)cortical structure relative to each other seem to follow a regular pattern. This intuition can be exploited to speed up detection and delineation of multiple anatomies: let $N \in \mathbb{N}^+$ be the number of structures that are about to be detected. Their hierarchical shape representation is

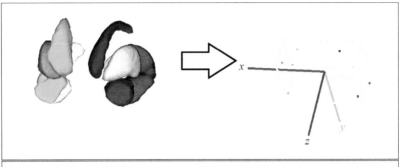

Figure 4.6: Composition of meta-structure for decreasing detection time.

shape (s_i, R_i, t_i, X_i) for $i \in \{1, \ldots, N\}$ as introduced above. We define a meta-structure $(\hat{s}, \hat{R}, \hat{t}, \hat{X})$ with

$$\hat{X} = (t_{1_1}, t_{1_2}, t_{1_3}, \ldots, t_{N_1}, t_{N_2}, t_{N_3})^T, \tag{4.20}$$

and $\hat{s}$, $\hat{R}$, and $\hat{t}$ estimated based on $\hat{X}$ via PCA as before. The process of meta-structure composition is exemplarily depicted in Fig. 4.6. The definition enables us to train a chain of discriminative models for rigid meta-structure detection in exactly the same way as it is done for rigid detection of any other (sub-)cortical gray matter structure. Again using GPA a population meta-structure mean shape can be computed based on the annotated training data at hand.

Instead of iteratively adapting an initial shape, that is, the mean shape, after it has been rigidly positioned according to the rigid detection's result $(\hat{s}^*, \hat{R}^*, \hat{t}^*)$, as done for shape inference, the very initial estimate of $\hat{X}^*$ is used to constrain subsequent position detection steps for individual anatomies. Position detection is then carried out exclusively on candidate voxels that fall within a certain radius about the meta-structure mean shape points $\hat{x}_i^*$, $i \in \{1, \ldots, N\}$.

The concept of meta-structure detection can be seen as an additional level of geometrical abstraction above the level of individual structures. The formal introduction of a recursive and therefore hierarchical MSL framework for multi-level rigid shape detection is beyond the scope of this chapter.

4.4 Validation

4.4.1 Material and Experimental Setup

For training and quantitative evaluation of our system there were four sets of T1-weighted MRI scans available (see Table 4.1). The first one is a subset of the "Designed Database of MR Brain Images of Healthy Volunteers"[1] [16] (DDHV) containing 20 scans. The associated ground-truth annotations were manually recovered from automatically generated segmentations [50] of the structures of interest. The second collection of 18 MRI scans was provided by the Center of Morphometric Analysis at the Massachusetts General Hospital and is publicly available on the Internet Brain Segmentation Repository[2] (IBSR 18). The scans are accompanied by detailed ground-truth annotations including the (sub-)cortical structures that are of interest here.[3] A subset[4] of the data provided by the "NIH MRI Study of Normal Brain Development"[5] consisiting of 10 pediatric data sets states another collection (NIH) of annotated MRI scans used for model generation. They have been manually annotated by the authors for training purposes. Additionally, we use data provided by the ongoing "3-D Segmentation in the Clinic: A Grand Challenge" competition[6] [56] for training and evaluation of the proposed method. The collection consists of several volumetric T1-weighted MRI brain scans of varying spatial resolution and size from multiple sources. The vast majority of data (29 scans) has been provided by the Psychiatry Neuroimaging Laboratory (PNL) at the Brigham and Women's Hospital (BWH), Boston. The other 20 data sets arose from a pediatric study, a Parkinson's Disease study, and a test/retest study carried out at the University of North Carolina's (UNC) Neuro Image Analysis Laboratory (NIAL), Chapel Hill. Only scans BWH PNL 1–15 (MICCAI'07 training) are accompanied by expert annotations for the left and right caudate nucleus, whereas for all the other data sets (MICCAI'07 testing) the ground-truth annotations of those two structures are held back by the providers. A predefined evaluation protocol is carried out fully

---

[1]The database was collected and made available by the CASILab at the University of North Carolina, Chapel Hill. The images were distributed by the MIDAS Data Server at Kitware, Inc. (insight-journal.org/midas)

[2]www.cma.mgh.harvard.edu/ibsr

[3]We corrected the ground-truth annotations for the left and the right caudate in the IBSR 18 data set to better meet the protocol applied by the "3-D Segmentation in the Clinic: A Grand Challenge" competition where the caudate is grouped with the nucleus accumbens in the delineations [56, 6].

[4]The following 10 data sets were used: defaced_native_100{2,3,7}_V{1,2}_t1w_r2, defaced_native_100{1,4,8}_V2_t1w_r2, and defaced_native_1005_V2_t1w_r2.

[5]The "NIH MRI Study of Normal Brain Development" is a multi-site, longitudinal study of typically developing children, from ages newborn through young adulthood, conducted by the Brain Development Cooperative Group and supported by the NICHD, the NIDA, the NIMH, and the NINDS (Contract #s N01-HD02-3343, N01-MH9-0002, and N01-NS-9-2314, -2315, -2316, -2317, -2319 and -2320). A listing of the participating sites and a complete listing of the study investigators can be found at www.bic.mni.mcgill.ca/nihpd/info/participating_centers.html. This manuscript reflects the view of the author and may not reflect the opinions or views of the NIH.

[6]www.cause07.org

automatically after uploading the testing fraction of the data to the Cause'07 file server. Evaluation is supposed to happen independently of any segmentation system developers in order to prevent over-adaptation to the testing data sets provided. First of all, the results are quantitatively evaluated on the BWH PNL scans 16–29, which are all considered to be routine scans, on 5 of the pediatric scans, and on 5 scans of patients older than 55 years (see Tables 4.3 and 4.4). Additionally, a system's accuracy is tested on 10 datasets of the same young healthy person acquired within 60 days on 5 different scanners (see Table 4.6). The COV of the volumetric measurements is an indicator on how stable the method operates in a test/re-test situation including scanner variability. We refer to [45, 56] and Appendix B for details on the used evaluation measures and to reference [56] for details on the used scoring system.

| | DDHV | IBSR 18 | NIH | MICCAI'07 | |
				training	testing
Volume Size	$176\times256\times160$	$256\times256\times128$	$124\times256\times256$, $176\times256\times256$, $160\times256\times256$	$256\times124\times156$ $256\times192\times256$	$256\times256\times198$, $256\times124\times256$, $176\times256\times160$,
Voxel Spacing (mm^3)	$1.0\times1.0\times1.0$	$0.84\times0.84\times1.5$, $0.94\times0.94\times1.5$, $1.0\times1.0\times1.5$	$1.3\times0.94\times0.94$, $1.5\times0.94\times0.94$, $1.5\times0.98\times0.98$, $1.4\times1.02\times1.02$	$0.94\times1.5\times0.94$	$0.94\times0.94\times0.94.0$, $0.94\times1.5\times0.94$, $1.0\times1.0\times1.0$, $1.02\times1.02\times1.02$
Sequence	T1	T1	T1	T1	T1
Number of Scans	20	18	10	15	24
Gound-truth	Yes	Yes	Yes	Yes	No

Table 4.1: Summary of the publicly available standard data used for model generation and evaluation purposes.

All the images were re-oriented to a uniform orientation ("RAI"; right-to-left, anterior-to-posterior, inferior-to-superior) and resampled to isotropic voxel spacing ($1.0\times1.0\times1.0$ mm^3) for processing. For increasing the amount of training data we exploited natural brain symmetry and therefore doubled the size of any training data set used for model generation by mirroring all the data sets with respect to the mid-sagittal plane. Throughout all our experiments we ensured that training and testing data are mutually exclusive: we trained models on all the available annotated data but left out IBSR 18 1–9 and IBSR 18 10-18 in turn for testing. As a result of not having any accompanying ground-truth annotations MICCAI'07 testing was never part of the training data.

As stated in reference [56] there are differences in the annotation protocols used for annotating the caudate nuclei in data sets originating from the BWH and the UNC. In the former the "tail" of the caudate is continued much further dorsally. We therefore decided to detect it as a separate structure that can be attached to the caudate nucleus if required. We did not try to automatically determine the annotation protocol used from the imaging data itself as this may lead to over-fitted systems. Moreover, in contrast to Tu et al. [109], we

Structure	Overlap Err. [%]	Dice Coeff. [%]	Volume Diff. [%]	Abs. Dist. [mm]	RMS Dist. [mm]	Max. Dist. [mm]
Left/right caudate nucleus	32.42	80.49	9.57	0.67	1.10	7.76
Left/right hippocampus	41.96	73.34	21.14	0.91	1.33	6.34
Left/right globus pallidus	39.72	74.97	20.97	0.79	1.24	5.53
Left/right putamen	29.82	82.37	13.76	0.72	1.15	6.60

Table 4.2: Average segmentation accuracy for IBSR 18 of models trained from mutually exclusive training and test data.

did not build models based on disjoint training data sets, which may be another cause for over-fitting.

As our real discriminative models are not ideal as assumed for theoretical considerations we keep the top 100 candidates after position detection and the top 25 candidates after position-orientation detection for further processing steps in order to make the full similarity transformation detection more robust. For our shape models we sampled the shapes of the 8 (sub-)cortical structures of interest with $n = 402$ surface points for the caudate and the hippocampus and with $n = 322$ surface points for the remaining structures. Subspace projection of the ASMs is constrained by $m = 46$ eigenvectors for all structures according to Zheng et al.'s [131] aforementioned heuristic. For shape inference we use $T = 3$ iterations.

In an optimized and parallelized C++ implementation of our segmentation method it takes about 5–10 seconds to detect and segment each (sub-)cortical structure in an MRI volume on a Fujitsu Siemens notebook equipped with an Intel Core 2 Duo CPU (2.20 GHz) and 3 GB of memory. Intensity standardization takes 1–2 seconds. The overall timing, without meta-structure detection, is comparable to the graph shifts algorithm [27] (50 seconds for 8 structures) and better than the auto context model (ACM) approach [77] (60 seconds for 1 structure), the hybrid discriminative/generative approach [109] (8 min. for 8 structures), and the method of Chupin et al. [20].

4.4.2 Quantitative Results

As can be seen from Table 4.2 in terms of the Dice coefficient our method achieves better results (80%,73%,75%,82%) for the segmentation of the caudate nuclei, hippocampi, globi pallidi, and putamina on the same IBSR 18 data set than the methods of Akselrod-Ballin et al. [2] (80%, 69%, 74%, 79%) and Gouttard et al. [50] (76%,67%,71%,78%) except for the caudate nuclei in reference [2], where we reach a comparable accuracy. It also reaches a higher score for the caudate nuclei and putamina on IBSR 18 than the method of Bazin and Pham [6] (78%,81%), which does not address segmentation of the hippocampi and globi pallidi. Fig. 4.7 gives a visual impression of the results obtained on IBSR 18.

Cases	Overlap Err. [%]	Score	Volume Diff. [%]	Score	Abs. Dist. [mm]	Score	RMS Dist. [mm]	Score	Max. Dist. [mm]	Score	Total Score
UNC Ped 10	25.86	83.74	4.88	91.43	0.60	77.84	1.18	78.85	10.36	69.54	80.28
UNC Ped 14	23.73	85.08	-0.56	99.02	0.47	82.68	0.83	85.11	5.80	82.93	86.96
UNC Ped 15	25.76	83.80	9.80	82.81	0.59	78.14	1.02	81.81	7.00	79.41	81.20
UNC Ped 19	30.30	80.94	-8.78	84.60	0.65	76.08	1.00	82.09	4.69	86.20	81.98
UNC Ped 30	28.77	81.91	4.66	91.83	0.63	76.65	1.03	81.58	6.81	79.98	82.39
UNC Eld 01	58.98	62.90	18.25	67.98	1.44	46.66	1.85	67.01	6.38	81.24	65.16
UNC Eld 12	35.79	77.49	43.78	23.19	0.79	70.56	1.14	79.68	5.05	85.14	67.21
UNC Eld 13	33.30	79.06	17.86	68.66	0.70	73.99	1.03	81.58	5.15	84.85	77.63
UNC Eld 20	28.48	82.09	17.75	68.87	0.63	76.67	1.09	80.53	9.35	72.51	76.13
UNC Eld 26	43.14	72.87	40.87	28.30	0.95	64.94	1.37	75.55	6.16	81.90	64.71
BWH PNL 16	39.27	75.30	-24.62	56.80	1.60	40.67	4.60	17.90	34.02	0.62	38.26
BWH PNL 17	33.14	79.15	-22.83	59.94	1.36	49.75	4.34	22.57	34.75	2.51	42.78
BWH PNL 18	34.44	78.34	-20.96	63.22	1.17	56.68	2.70	51.83	19.04	44.01	58.82
BWH PNL 19	34.47	78.32	-7.38	87.06	1.27	52.87	3.52	37.13	29.85	12.20	53.52
BWH PNL 20	33.60	78.87	0.79	98.61	1.07	60.38	3.38	39.65	33.35	2.05	55.91
BWH PNL 21	41.34	74.00	-27.02	52.60	1.80	33.47	4.55	18.69	34.73	0.00	35.75
BWH PNL 22	39.85	74.94	-26.38	53.72	1.35	50.18	3.56	36.37	29.24	13.99	45.84
BWH PNL 23	28.98	81.77	-10.88	80.91	0.81	70.18	2.15	61.59	18.77	44.80	67.85
BWH PNL 24	28.86	81.85	-9.44	83.44	0.74	72.52	1.74	68.91	14.18	58.29	73.00
BWH PNL 25	32.91	79.30	7.43	86.97	1.33	50.80	3.83	31.61	30.85	9.27	51.59
BWH PNL 26	43.12	72.88	-15.38	73.01	1.06	60.62	2.05	63.33	13.61	59.96	65.96
BWH PNL 27	28.25	82.23	-8.48	85.12	1.48	45.24	4.74	15.29	32.80	3.53	46.28
BWH PNL 28	34.30	78.43	-23.58	58.63	1.43	46.97	4.36	22.07	30.99	8.86	42.99
BWH PNL 29	33.83	78.72	-1.74	92.92	0.88	67.40	1.87	66.54	16.19	52.39	71.59
Average UNC Ped	26.88	83.09	2.00	89.94	0.59	78.28	1.01	81.89	6.93	79.61	82.56
Average UNC Eld	39.94	74.88	27.70	51.40	0.90	66.57	1.30	76.87	6.42	81.13	70.17
Average BWH PNL	34.74	78.15	-13.61	73.78	1.24	54.12	3.39	39.53	26.60	22.32	53.58
Average All	34.19	78.50	-1.75	72.49	1.03	61.75	2.46	56.14	18.30	46.51	63.08

Table 4.3: Average left/right caudate segmentation accuracy for the MICCAI'07 testing data set without optional caudate tail detection. As of 02/25/2009 this method ranks number 11 in the overall ranking list on www.cause07.org ("LME Erlangen").

The overall average score (75.19) in Table 4.4 shows that for segmenting the caudate nuclei our method performs better than the methods of Morra et al. [77] (73.38), Bazin and Pham [6] (64.73) and Tu et al. [109] (59.71). All the mentioned authors report on results computed on the same MICCAI'07 testing data set. In fact, our method with integrated caudate tail tip detection ranks number 2 in the overall ranking list on www.cause07.org ("Segmentation Team") as of 03/10/2009.

4.5   Discussion

One of the limiting aspects of our extended MSL method is the fact that all the patient data sets we used for model generation origin from patients not being affected by pathologies

Cases	Overlap Err. [%]	Score	Volume Diff. [%]	Score	Abs. Dist. [mm]	Score	RMS Dist. [mm]	Score	Max. Dist. [mm]	Score	Total Score
UNC Ped 10	29.87	81.22	17.06	70.08	0.64	76.38	1.05	81.22	7.18	78.88	77.55
UNC Ped 14	31.55	80.16	7.48	86.87	0.85	68.53	1.89	66.18	15.82	53.48	71.05
UNC Ped 15	25.66	83.86	5.55	90.26	0.58	78.36	1.10	80.28	10.30	69.72	80.50
UNC Ped 19	24.66	84.49	4.22	92.59	0.65	75.80	1.51	73.03	13.33	60.80	77.34
UNC Ped 30	24.83	84.39	1.90	93.72	0.50	81.31	0.88	84.23	7.02	79.34	84.60
UNC Eld 01	40.31	74.65	14.92	73.83	0.93	65.39	1.62	71.05	13.18	61.24	69.23
UNC Eld 12	33.13	79.16	12.60	77.89	0.72	73.23	1.37	75.46	12.38	63.57	73.86
UNC Eld 13	29.09	81.71	5.83	89.77	0.57	78.92	0.97	82.71	9.46	72.18	81.06
UNC Eld 20	32.23	79.73	12.25	78.51	0.65	75.83	1.01	81.92	6.90	79.72	79.14
UNC Eld 26	37.64	76.33	8.05	85.88	0.79	70.72	1.58	71.80	15.95	53.09	71.56
BWH PNL 16	37.12	76.65	-26.96	52.71	0.65	75.79	1.08	80.73	8.51	74.96	72.17
BWH PNL 17	27.83	82.50	-12.83	77.50	0.49	82.01	0.91	83.75	6.24	81.66	81.48
BWH PNL 18	30.31	80.94	-23.71	58.41	0.60	77.88	1.06	81.00	10.60	68.82	73.41
BWH PNL 19	33.96	78.64	-11.82	79.26	0.70	74.11	1.20	78.66	8.07	76.28	77.39
BWH PNL 20	29.52	81.43	-8.94	84.31	0.51	81.26	0.91	83.81	6.61	80.56	82.28
BWH PNL 21	40.36	74.61	-34.83	38.89	0.89	66.92	1.46	73.89	10.30	69.72	64.81
BWH PNL 22	38.96	75.50	-30.52	46.46	0.79	70.62	1.20	78.63	8.48	75.07	69.25
BWH PNL 23	29.45	81.48	-8.69	84.75	0.78	70.94	2.25	59.83	21.33	37.26	66.85
BWH PNL 24	24.30	84.72	-6.49	88.62	0.45	83.32	0.91	83.71	13.70	59.69	80.01
BWH PNL 25	29.33	81.55	-6.12	89.27	0.81	69.86	2.18	61.03	21.43	36.97	67.73
BWH PNL 26	34.45	78.34	-24.77	56.54	0.65	75.84	1.30	76.70	14.69	56.81	68.84
BWH PNL 27	25.99	83.65	-13.91	75.59	0.53	80.30	1.01	81.93	6.48	80.94	80.48
BWH PNL 28	34.00	78.62	-22.87	59.87	0.64	76.20	1.13	79.81	6.85	79.86	74.87
BWH PNL 29	28.47	82.09	0.87	90.60	0.54	80.14	0.99	82.29	13.39	60.62	79.15
Average UNC Ped	27.31	82.82	7.24	86.70	0.65	76.08	1.29	76.99	10.73	68.44	78.21
Average UNC Eld	34.48	78.31	10.73	81.18	0.73	72.82	1.31	76.59	11.57	65.96	74.97
Average BWH PNL	31.72	80.05	-16.54	70.20	0.65	76.08	1.26	77.56	11.19	67.09	74.20
Average All	31.38	80.27	-5.91	75.92	0.66	75.40	1.27	77.24	11.17	67.14	75.19

Table 4.4: Average left/right caudate segmentation accuracy for the MICCAI'07 testing data set with optional caudate tail detection. As of 03/10/2009 this method ranks number 2 in the overall ranking list on www.cause07.org ("Segmentation Team").

disturbing the usual composition and appearance of the human brain's anatomy in a, from a medical imaging perspective, serious manner. For instance, there are not any intracranial mass lesions such as tumors, abscesses, or hemorrhages deforming the surrounding tissue. This may lead to a decreased robustness of the system against this kind of pathological changes in the human brain and may yield sub-optimal results in such cases. From our point of view there are two ways to overcome this issue: first, one could try to increase the amount of training data and therefore allowing the involved models to also capture pathological abnormalities. Second, one could try to implement recovering strategies in case deforming pathologies prevent proper detection of anatomies.

Aiming for comparable validation results we evaluated our approach on two publicly available databases (IBSR 18 and MICCAI'07 testing) for the caudate nucleus and on one

Correlation	UNC Ped	UNC Eld	BWH PNL	Total
Left	0.53	0.94	0.65	0.71
Right	0.63	0.95	0.50	0.69
Average	0.58	0.79	0.58	0.70

Table 4.5: Pearson correlation for the volume measurements in the three testing groups as well as in total. This coefficient captures how well the volumetric measurements correlate with those of the reference segmentations.

Test/Re-Test		Left	Right	Total
UNC 03	[mm^3]	3745	3714	7459
UNC 04	[mm^3]	3950	3781	7731
UNC 09	[mm^3]	3906	4011	7918
UNC 11	[mm^3]	3871	3822	7693
UNC 17	[mm^3]	3751	3735	7486
UNC 18	[mm^3]	3935	3988	7923
UNC 21	[mm^3]	3765	3714	7479
UNC 22	[mm^3]	4047	3782	7829
UNC 24	[mm^3]	4142	3770	7912
UNC 25	[mm^3]	2783	3119	5902
Mean	[mm^3]	3790	3744	7533
Stdev	[mm^3]	357	231	572
COV	[%]	9.0	6.0	8.0

Table 4.6: The volumetric measurements of the 10 data sets of the same young adult acquired on 5 different scanners within 60 days. The COV indicates the stability of the algorithm in a test/re-test situation including scanner variability.

publicly available databases (IBSR 18) for all the other (sub-)cortical gray matter structures. Both IBSR 18 and MICCAI'07 testing have been established to allow objective comparison of segmentation methods. Especially the web-based evaluation of results on MICCAI'07 testing is designed to validate accuracy and robustness of segmentation approaches.

Though better than recently reported results, or at least comparable, a Dice coefficient of, for instance, 73% for the hippocampus might be considered too low for reliable volumetric studies from a clinical perspective. Some methods [77, 20, 55, 85] reach higher scores for certain structures when evaluated on non-publicly available data sets. However, comparability to scores computed on different databases is limited due to different characteristics of the data with respect to MRI artifacts and pathology. The typical MRI artifacts, such as Rician noise [80], PVEs [114], and intra-/inter-scan INUs [119, 60], might be there in a more or less distinctive manner. Also, as mentioned above, the presence of pathology may significantly affect the achievable segmentation accuracy on a particular database. From our point of view, objective comparison of segmentation methods is only possible by using publicly available benchmark databases.

With respect to the achieved overall score on MICCAI'07 testing our method (~75), as well as all the others presented in the overall ranking at www.cause07.org as of 05/20/2009, still fails to keep up with the score (~90) presumed typical for a human expert when manually delineating the left and right caudate nucleus [56]. The decision to assign an overall score of approximately 90 to the segmentation accuracy achievable by an independent human observer was based on preliminary tests [56].

In comparison to registration-based approaches working with anatomical atlases [94, 6, 2, 85] exhaustive labeling of all the anatomical structures in the human brain independently from each other with our extended MSL framework may become a lengthy undertaking on today's hardware—even though processing is comparably fast for a manageable amount of anatomies. Exploiting geometrical knowledge about the anatomies and their relation to each other, like already done by introducing meta-structure detection, even on the level of common boundaries may help to overcome this drawback of the current system. While currently only the translation search ranges for individual anatomies are constrained by meta-structure detection this may be extended by also constraining search ranges for orientation and scaling. However, this may be at the risk of propagating detection errors from one level of geometrical abstraction to the one beneath.

Another critical point is the considerable amount of annotated training data necessary to generate robust models for the presented approach. Zheng et al. [131, 130] evaluate their MSL approach on more than 300 CT volume data sets in a cross validation setup. Ling et al. [71] work with almost 200 CT scans. Yet, the amount of available training data can be easily augmented by suitable annotation tools allowing to correct automatically generated annotations generated by systems trained on less data.

In the current system all the parameters for training rigid detection are estimated based on the shape information itself. There are not any characteristic anatomical landmarks of a high recognition factor, both facilitating manual labeling as well as fully automatic detection, used for deriving the associated local coordinate systems. Only for the detection and segmentation of the caudate nuclei the approximated centerline used for mesh re-sampling is unilaterally bounded by the manually annotated tail tip. Paying respect to anatomical characteristics in defining such landmarks may improve the overall accuracy of the system in certain cases [130, 131]. The ease of defining appropriate landmarks depends on the addressed segmentation scenario.

The system presented is comparably fast: without meta-structure detection it takes only 1–2 minutes to segment 8 (sub-)cortical gray matter structures. Processing time can be decreased to on average 13.9 seconds by means of meta-structure detection. This makes our approach even preferable to the method of Corso et al. [28], which is found to be the fastest in our literature research.

In comparison to Zheng et al. [130, 131] we give a slightly different, though sound, mathematical formulation of an extended MSL approach that also integrates shape inference. We show that MSL naturally decomposes the search space along levels of geometrical abstraction successively refining anatomy representation. This allows the use of a chain of discriminative models. As machine learning-, and therefore knowledge-based, approaches are used on every level of abstraction, the method is entirely top-down—not only from a geometrical but also from a methodological point of view. Knowledge is incorporated into the system by exploiting a large database of expert-annotated training data for model generation, which aligns the method with the paradigm of database-guided medical image segmentation [44].

4.6 Conclusions

The contributions of this chapter are as follows: we integrated shape inference into the overall MSL methodology from the theoretical point of view. We showed that MSL decomposes the parameter space of anatomy shapes along decreasing levels of geometrical abstraction into subspaces of increasing dimensionality and applied MSL to the difficult problem of (sub-)cortical gray matter structure detection and shape inference. Experiments on publicly available gold standard databases show that our method works equally fast, robust, and accurate at a state-of-the-art level.

In the following chapter we will summarize the core contributions of this thesis. We will also discuss general technological and methodological considerations, give a brief outlook on future work, and draw conclusions.

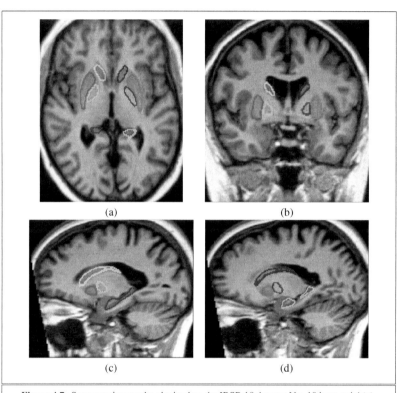

(a)   (b)

(c)   (d)

Figure 4.7: Segmentation results obtained on the IBSR 18 data set No. 10 in an axial (a), coronal (b), and right (c) and left (d) sagittal view. The segmented structures are the left and right caudate (dark-blue/yellow), the left and right putamen (orange/blue), the left and right globus pallidus (green/red), and the left and right hippocampus (turquoise/violet).

Chapter 5

Summary and Outlook

5.1 Summary and Contributions

This thesis dealt with probabilistic modeling for segmentation of the human brain and related structures from MRI data. The human brain plays an important role in centrally controlling a vast majority of functions of the human body. Moreover, it hosts all aspects of human consciousness. This makes every disease infecting the human brain a critical issue that requires the newest and most accurate means of medical diagnostics and therapy available. Many diseases affect morphology and usual appearance of the human brain in radiological examinations. For its excellent soft tissue contrast MRI is the radiological modality of choice for imaging the human's central nervous system.

When it comes to the analysis of radiological images one usually wants to bridge the gap between sequences of signal measurements, which is what radiological 2-D images or 3-D images actually are, and a semantic description of what is depicted—one wants to "understand" the medical images at hand. Providing this understanding, that is to say, these semantics, can serve several purposes when dealing with radiological pictorial material: on the one hand they can be used for improved traditional medical decision making, i.e., medical diagnostics and therapy planning and monitoring. On the other hand, explicit semantics stored in a machine-readable format allow usage of the data and the patient-specific knowledge supplied herewith for higher level post-processing: computer-aided diagnostics and treatment planning and also retrospective studies of certain diseases and their progress may all be based on the automatic extraction of diagnostically relevant quantitative or more abstract findings. The research project Health-e-Child, wherein this work of research is embedded, is dedicated to this emerging field within medical informatics and covers pooling and intelligently post-processing semantically enriched medical data and storing general medical knowledge in the context of pediatrics. Finally, explicit semantics can even be used for knowledge-based image enhancement as exemplified in Chapter 2.

Throughout this thesis we examined ways to provide explicit semantics for medical imaging data by means of medical image segmentation and labeling, which is a standard methodology for the problem of partly understanding medical images. We exemplified this general approach to the problem by developing and successfully applying three new methods from the field of database-guided knowledge-based approaches for three distinct medical image segmentation scenarios: 3-D MRI brain tissue classification and INU correction, pediatric brain tumor segmentation in multi-spectral 3-D MRI, and 3-D MRI brain structure segmentation. Together, all the three chosen scenarios cover a broader range of how the human brain's morphology and usual condition can be affected by pathology. With regards to the results our methods achieve we can conclude that database-guided knowledge-based approaches, exemplified by the three developed methods of this thesis, are well-suited for the purpose of fully automatically generating semantic descriptions for medical imaging data.

For the first scenario we presented a fully automated method, that is, the DMC-EM algorithm, for brain tissue classification into GM, , and CSF regions and intra-scan INU correction in 3-D MR images. In its integrated multi-spectral Bayesian formulation based on the MRF methodology we could combine supervised MRI modality-specific discriminative modeling and unsupervised EM segmentation. The MRF regularization involved took into account knowledge about spatial and appearance related homogeneity of segments using pair-wise clique potentials and patient-specific knowledge about the global spatial distribution of brain tissue using PBT-based unary clique potentials. The PBT features used rely on surrounding context and alignment-based features derived from a pre-registered probabilistic anatomical atlas. The context considered is encoded by 3-D Haar-like features of reduced INU sensitivity. Our detailed quantitative evaluations on standard phantom scans and standard real world data showed the accuracy and robustness of the proposed method. By comparison with other state-of-the-art approaches we were able to demonstrate our method's relative superiority with regards to the chosen medical imaging scenario.

In the second scenario, we addressed fully automatic pediatric brain tumor segmentation in multi-spectral 3-D MRI. The developed method, that is, the DMC-GC algorithm, is based on an MRF model that combines PBT discriminative modeling and lower-level segmentation via graph cuts. The PBT algorithm provides a prior model in terms of an external field classifying tumor appearance while a spatial prior takes into account pair-wise voxel homogeneities both in terms of classification labels as well as in terms of multi-spectral voxel intensities. As above the discriminative model relies not only on observed local intensities but also on surrounding context for detecting candidate regions for pathology. We were able to provide a mathematically sound formulation for integrating the two approaches into a unified statistical framework. In a quantitative evaluation we obtained results that were mostly better than those reported for current state-of-the-art approaches to 3-D MRI brain tumor segmentation.

The third and final scenario comprised 3-D MRI brain structure segmentation where we developed a novel method for the automatic detection and segmentation of (sub-)cortical GM structures in 3-D MR images of the human brain. The method is based on the MSL concept. We showed that MSL naturally decomposes the parameter space of anatomy shapes along decreasing levels of geometrical abstraction into subspaces of increasing dimensionality. This is done by exploiting parameter invariance. This insight allows us to build strong discriminative PBT models from annotated training data on each level of abstraction. During shape detection and inference the range of possible solutions is narrowed using these models until a final shape is found. We could extend the original MSL formalism to also cover shape inference and not only rigid shape detection. The segmentation accuracy achieved is mostly better than the one of other state-of-the-art approaches for (sub-)cortical GM structure segmentation. For benchmarking purposes, our method was evaluated on publicly available gold standard databases consisting of several T1-weighted 3-D brain MRI scans from different scanners and sites. The choice of images within these databases is guided by the intention to reflect the challenging environment a segmentation algorithm has to face when applied in clinical practice.

Next to these major contributions the following minor contribution was made: in the second and third scenario we adapted the DHW approach for 1-D histogram matching whose original purpose is ensuring constant image brightness in traditional gray scale images to mono-spectral MRI inter-scan intensity standardization. We gave a graph theoretic re-formulation of the algorithm and extended it to minimize the Kullback-Leibler divergence between 1-D histograms of equal bin size. Inter-scan intensity standardization is one of the prerequisites to the application of machine learning-based segmentation techniques relying directly or indirectly on observed image intensities.

5.2 Discussion and Technological Considerations

Although we discussed issues related to the particular systems and scenarios we presented at the end of each chapter there are some more general technological and methodological considerations and aspects that need to be mentioned.

With regards to the broader subject of semantic imaging we had to restrict our discourse on this matter to three well-defined MRI segmentation scenarios. A more general and more theoretical dealing with the fully automatic semantic analysis of medical pictorial material would have gone far beyond the scope of this work.

Due to the characteristics of the chosen scenarios we were limited to the analysis of static morphological points of view. The study of other medical imaging modalities for the purpose of semantic analysis, such as 3-D+t or functional imaging, is necessary to also address physiological and pathophysiological aspects of the human body. Also, we concentrated on the important first steps towards explicit semantics for medical imaging data—medical image segmentation and labeling. From our point of view, narrowing the topic that way appears reasonable in order to deal with it in a sufficiently concise manner that is in accordance with the ambition of this kind of scientific piece of writing.

From a technological point of view, focusing on database-guided knowledge-based approaches involving machine learning might also appear as if we unnecessarily imposed a restriction on the scope of this work. However, we found out from the literature that this methodology represents a current trend in today's medical image segmentation and that this kind of approaches is well-suited for semantic imaging purposes. An important question arises nevertheless: are the databases used for model-generation large enough to cover the large variety of possible deformations the human brain, as in our case, can be subject to? This is certainly questionable due to the almost unpredictable impact of possible malfunctions and diseases on morphology. On the other hand the investigation of pathology by radiological imaging is fundamental for medical inquiries. Encouraged by what is to be found in the literature and by the evaluation results of our methods we believe that sufficiently large databases can be chosen covering at least the common spectrum of possible deformations and changes in anatomical appearance also in the case of pathology.

Throughout this thesis we made extensively use of the PBT algorithm (see Appendix A) for machine learning. The technique is closely related to the cascade approach of Viola and Jones [115]. Though generic in formulation the PBT algorithm is usually used in combination with AdaBoost [41] as strong classifier within each tree node. As a matter of fact, PBT is still lacking a detailed analysis from a theoretical point of view revealing its robustness against over-fitting and effects of certain parameter settings. A comparison with other boosting strategies, such as random forests [12] or pure AdaBoost, would definitely be worth investigation. As we approached involved technologies from the entire medical image segmentation scenario's point of view we did not have the ambition to evaluate all imaginable design choices concerning our methods. However, most of the design choices are well founded in the literature.

Where possible we decided to evaluate our approaches on publicly available gold standard data sets. Even though this ensures comparability of different methods, researchers relying on these data sets are at the risk of another subtle methodological error: "training on the test data" [35, 56] . It is the case when a classifier or method undergoes a longer series of refinements, which are guided by repeated experiments on the same test data. As some of the used benchmarking databases have been persisting in the public domain for quite some time the best-performing methods may be over-adapted to specific characteristics of these data collections. These characteristics may not represent the general case of a particular medical image segmentation scenario. This disadvantage was addressed by Heimann et al. [56] with their onsite segmentation contest at MICCAI 2007 in Brisbane, Australia, and their ongoing online caudate segmentation challenge (www.cause07.org).

In the contest, the final evaluation was carried out on a third set of previously unseen data sets that were not distributed to the participants with the training and testing data. From the opposite point of view, due to the limited number of data sets available, the question arises whether these collections reflect the possible spectrum of challenges that can be associated with a certain segmentation scenario. Another aspect is "saturation" meaning that new methods are likely to only achieve marginal improvements on benchmarking data sets that have already been used for evaluation purposes by many researchers. In this case significant improvements are almost impossible. However, we are convinced that evaluation on publicly available gold standard or benchmarking data sets is one of the best ways to objectively compare methods as, despite the aforementioned objections, every method faces the same replicable prerequisites.

Most often we carried out benchmarking by comparing complete systems. This means we assessed methods on the highest level of abstraction with respect to their processing pipeline and compared their final segmentation results. This aligns with our ambition to approach medical imaging scenarios from an integral perspective rather than from a pure technological perspective with focus restricted in terms of technological categories. Usually, we did not evaluate individual processing steps separately.

Typically there was only one ground-truth annotation per dataset available both for training as well as for evaluation of all the three scenarios' systems. Therefore, we could not study any intra- and inter-observer variability this being a limitation of the data sets at hand.

Even though addressed to some extend computational performance of our systems was not one of the major aspects of this work. Improvements may be possible due to new hardware developments and more elaborated implementations properly exploiting present and future hard- and software capabilities.

5.3 Future Work

As mentioned above enriching medical imaging content with semantic annotations of any kind is an emerging field in today's medical informatics research. Future work on this topic will have to address, but is not limited to, the following scientific questions:

- Which kind of features should semantics be generated from? Step-wise along a chain of explicit semantic descriptors, which are also understandable to humans, or immediately from the signal measurements by means of classical low-level feature extraction and pattern recognition-style classification?

- How can semantics be intelligently integrated into applications of added value? How would these applications look like? How can they make use of distributed sources of semantic content over the internet?

- How can these applications be kept scalable despite the huge amount medical imaging data generated every day all over the world? Both with regards to the processing as wells as to the generation of semantic content.

- How can the clinical workflow benefit from semantic annotations in medical imaging data?

- Are there ways to flexibly combine semantics generated from different sources of data within a field of knowledge? Which formal representations should be chosen for this purpose?

Next to these more general inquiries there are also possibilities for future research dealing directly with the three medical imaging scenarios we concentrated on and the associated methods we proposed. They include, but are not restricted to, the following questions:

- Can the methods be applied to other body regions and other imaging modalities?

- How can robustness against disease-related changes in morphology be increased?

- How do different design choices in terms of low-level image features or techniques, for instance, other machine learning techniques, affect the accuracy and performance of the methods?

- Can more complicated shapes like, for example, the entire cerebral cortex be addressed by similar methods?

- Can the methods be made more MRI-specific by feeding knowledge about the MR image acquisition back into the segmentation process?

5.4   Conclusions

In this work, we addressed probabilistic modeling for segmentation in MR images of the human brain in three distinct scenarios. In all scenarios, we concentrated on database-guided knowledge-based approaches that make use of machine learning in order to provide probabilistic models. We could show that our newly developed, fully automatic approaches are well-suited for the problem of providing explicit semantics for medical imaging data in terms of labeled image regions. Regarding the methodologies applied, major and minor advances in research could be made as summarized above. Both from our work as well as from what can be found in the literature we conclude that database-guided knowledge-based approaches are at the point of becoming the state-of-the-art in medical image segmentation. They successfully combine traditional medical imaging with machine learning and pattern recognition techniques.

Appendix A

Discriminative Modeling

A.1 Probabilistic Boosting-Trees

Training a probabilistic boosting-tree (PBT) (see Fig. A.1) resembles inducing a multivariate binary decision tree from a set of weighted labeled training examples $\mathcal{T} = \{(z_n, y_n, w_n) \mid n = 1, \ldots, N\} \in \mathcal{T}$, $N \in \mathbb{N}$, with feature vectors $z_n \in \mathcal{Z} = \mathbb{R}^M$, $M \in \mathbb{N}$, labels $y_n \in \{-1, +1\}$, and weights $w_n \in [0, 1]$ with $\sum_{n=1}^{N} w_n = 1$. Within each node v of the tree a strong discriminative model $H_v(z) \in (-1, +1)$ for feature vectors $z \in \mathbb{R}^M$, $M \in \mathbb{N}$, is generated. By construction, all those models $H(z)$ asymptotically approach an additive logistic regression model [42]

$$H(z) \approx \frac{1}{2} \ln \frac{p(y = +1|z)}{p(y = -1|z)} \tag{A.1}$$

where $y \in \{-1, +1\}$ denotes the outcome of the associated binary classification task. Accordingly, at each node v of the resulting PBT there are current approximations of the posterior probabilities $\tilde{p}_v(+1|z) = q_v(z) = \exp(2H(z))/(1 + \exp(2H(z)))$ and $\tilde{p}_v(-1|z) = 1 - q_v(z)$. During classification those values are used to guide tree traversing and combined propagation of posteriors in order to get a final approximation $\tilde{p}(y|z)$ of the true posterior probability $p(y|z)$ at the tree's root node.

While training the classifier, those probabilities are used to successively split the set of training data relative to the prior probability $p_v(y = +1)$ associated with the current training (sub-)set in node v into two new subsets. We write p_v instead of $p_v(y = +1)$ in the following for simplicity. The soft thresholding parameter $\epsilon > 0$ sees to pass on training samples z that are close to the current node's decision boundary, that is to say, if $q_v(z) \in [(1 - \epsilon)p_v; (1 + \epsilon)p_v]$, to both of the resulting subsets and associated subtrees. See Algorithm 4 for details on how a PBT is built.

During classification the values for $q_v(z)$ are used to guide tree traversing and combined propagation of posteriors in order to get final approximations $\tilde{p}_v(y|z)$ of the true posterior

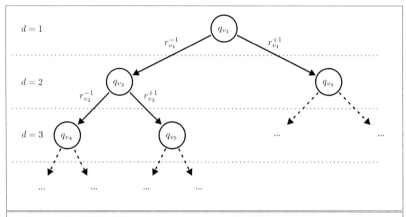

Figure A.1: A PBT with a strong discriminative probabilistic model in each tree node.

probabilities $p_v(y|z)$ at each tree node v: for outgoing edges r_v^{-1} and r_v^1 associated with the possible classifications the approximation $\tilde{p}_v(y|z)$ can be computed via the recursive formula

$$\tilde{p}_v(y|z) = \begin{cases} \tilde{p}_{\beta(r_v^{-1})}(y|z) & \text{if } q_v(z) < (1-\epsilon)p_v, \\ \tilde{p}_{\beta(r_v^{+1})}(y|z) & \text{if } q_v(z) > (1+\epsilon)p_v, \\ \sum_i \tilde{p}_{\beta(r_v^i)}(y|z) \cdot q_v(i|z) & \text{otherwise,} \end{cases} \tag{A.2}$$

where $\beta(r)$ denotes the vertex where edge r ends and $q_v(+1|z) = q_v(z)$ and $q_v(-1|z) = 1 - q_v(z)$.

A.2   AdaBoost

Probabibilistic boosting-trees can be built in combination with several strong learning algorithms providing the strong classifier within each tree node. In the following we give a concise description of the most commonly used one, which is AdaBoost [41]. It is called Discrete AdaBoost by Friedman et al. [42]. In the two-class classification setting we have a set $\mathcal{T} = \{ (z_n, y_n, w_n) \mid n = 1, \ldots, N \} \in \mathcal{T}$ of weighted labeled training data, $N \in \mathbb{N}$, with feature vectors $z_n \in \mathcal{Z} = \mathbb{R}^M$, $M \in \mathbb{N}$, labels $y_n \in \{ -1, +1 \}$, and weights $w_n = 1/N$. The purpose of Discrete AdaBoost is to find a strong classifier

$$H(z) = \sum_{t=1}^{T} \alpha_t h_t(z), \tag{A.3}$$

that is, a linear combination of $T \in \mathbb{N}$ weak classifiers $h_t(z)$ giving hard classification outcomes with weights $\alpha_t \in \mathbb{R}$; the corresponding prediction of this strong classifier is $\mathrm{sgn}(H(z))$. The procedure builds weak classifiers on weighted training samples in turn giving higher weight to those that are currently misclassified (see Fig. A.2). A detailed description of Discrete AdaBoost is given in Algorithm 5.

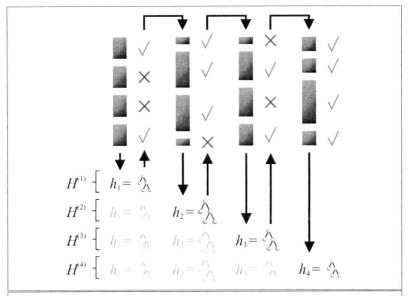

Figure A.2: Schematic representation of $T = 4$ iterations of the Discrete AdaBoost algorithm. The strong classifier available at the end of each iteration $t = 1, \ldots, T$ is denoted by $H^{(t)}$.

For the purpose of discriminative brain tissue modeling, we use a generalized version of AdaBoost, which is called Real AdaBoost [42] (see Algorithm 6). One of the major differences to Discrete AdaBoost is the fact that the weak learners return class probability estimates $f(z) = p(y = +1|z)$ instead of hard classifications. We generate class probability estimates by means of decision stumps, which are inductively learned decision trees of depth 1, returning the probability distributions of $y \in \{-1, +1\}$ after only one split of a training data set $\mathcal{T}$. A split is found by choosing a feature vector component z_m and an accompanying threshold θ_m that "best" separates the positive from the negative samples. We refer to Quinlan [90] for details on this.

Algorithm 4: PBT

Input: set of weighted labeled training examples $\mathcal{T} = \{ (z_n, y_n, w_n) \mid n = 1, \ldots, N \} \in \mathbf{T}$, $N \in \mathbb{N}$,
    with feature vectors $z_n \in \mathcal{Z} = \mathbb{R}^M$, $M \in \mathbb{N}$, labels $y_n \in \{ -1, +1 \}$, and weights
    $w_n \in [0, 1]$, $\sum_{n=1}^{N} w_n = 1$, a strong discriminative probability estimator
    $L : \mathbf{T} \times \mathbb{N} \to \{ f : \mathcal{Z} \to (0, 1) \text{ with } f(z) = p(y = +1|z) \}$, the number of weak classifiers
    $S \in \mathbb{N}$ per tree node, the current tree depth $d \in \mathbb{N}$ (initially $d = 0$), and the maximum tree
    depth $D \in \mathbb{N}$

Output: Probabilistic Boosting-Tree node

begin
    Let v be the current tree node;

    // Compute the empirical distribution
    $p_v \leftarrow \sum_{n=1}^{N} w_n \delta(+1, y_n)$;

    // Train a strong discriminative model
    $q_v \leftarrow L[\mathcal{T}, S]$;

    // Initialize subsets
    if $d=D$ **then**
      | return v
    else
      Add new tree nodes $\beta(r_v^{-1})$ and $\beta(r_v^{+1})$;
      $\mathcal{T}^{-1} = \emptyset$;
      $\mathcal{T}^{+1} = \emptyset$;
      for $n = 1, \ldots, N$ **do**
        if $q_v(z_n) < (1 - \epsilon)p_v$ **then**
        | $\mathcal{T}^{-1} \leftarrow \mathcal{T}^{-1} \cup \{ (z_n, y_n, w_n) \}$;
        else
          if $q_v(z_n) > (1 + \epsilon)p_v$ **then**
          | $\mathcal{T}^{+1} \leftarrow \mathcal{T}^{+1} \cup \{ (z_n, y_n, w_n) \}$;
          else
            $\mathcal{T}^{-1} \leftarrow \mathcal{T}^{-1} \cup \{ (z_n, y_n, w_n) \}$;
            $\mathcal{T}^{+1} \leftarrow \mathcal{T}^{+1} \cup \{ (z_n, y_n, w_n) \}$;
          end
        end
      end

      // Increase tree depth and normalize
      $d \leftarrow d + 1$;
      for $n = 1, \ldots, |\mathcal{T}^{-1}|$ **do**
      | $w_n \leftarrow w_n / (\sum_{n=1}^{|\mathcal{T}^{-1}|} w_n)$;
      end
      for $n = 1, \ldots, |\mathcal{T}^{+1}|$ **do**
      | $w_n \leftarrow w_n / (\sum_{n=1}^{|\mathcal{T}^{+1}|} w_n)$;
      end

      // Repeat procedure recursively
      $\beta(r_v^{-1}) \leftarrow PBT[\mathcal{T}^{-1}, L, S, d, D]$;
      $\beta(r_v^{+1}) \leftarrow PBT[\mathcal{T}^{+1}, L, S, d, D]$;

      return v;
    end
end

Algorithm 5: Discrete AdaBoost

Input: set of weighted labeled training examples $\mathcal{T} = \{\, (z_n, y_n, w_n) \mid n = 1, \ldots, N \,\} \in \boldsymbol{T}$, $N \in \mathbb{N}$, with feature vectors $z_n \in \mathcal{Z} = \mathbb{R}^M$, $M \in \mathbb{N}$, labels $y_n \in \{\, -1, +1 \,\}$, and weights $w_n = 1/N$, a weak learning algorithm $\boldsymbol{L} : \boldsymbol{T} \to \{\, h : \mathcal{Z} \to \{\, -1, +1 \,\} \,\}$, and the number of weak classifiers $T \in \mathbb{N}$

Output: strong classifier $H : \mathcal{Z} \to \mathbb{R}$ with $H(z) = \sum_{t=1}^{T} \alpha_t h_t(z)$

begin

    for $t = 1, \ldots, T$ **do**

        // Build weak classifier

        $h_t \leftarrow \boldsymbol{L}[\mathcal{T}]$;

        // Compute error rate

        $\epsilon \leftarrow 0$;

        for $n = 1, \ldots, N$ **do**

            if $h_t(x_n) \neq y_n$ **then**

                $\epsilon \leftarrow \epsilon + w_n$;

            end

        end

        // Adapt sample weights

        for $n = 1, \ldots, N$ **do**

            if $h_t(x_n) = y_n$ **then**

                $w_n \leftarrow w_n \cdot \epsilon/(1 - \epsilon)$;

            end

        end

        for $n = 1, \ldots, N$ **do**

            $w_n \leftarrow w_n / (\sum_{n=1}^{N} w_n)$;

        end

        // Compute weights of weak classifiers

        $\alpha_m \leftarrow \log \frac{1 - \epsilon}{\epsilon}$;

    end

    return $H(z) = \sum_{t=1}^{T} \alpha_t h_t(z)$;

end

Algorithm 6: Real AdaBoost

Input: set of weighted labeled training examples $\mathcal{T} = \{ (z_n, y_n, w_n) \mid n = 1, \ldots, N \} \in \mathbf{T}$, $N \in \mathbb{N}$, with feature vectors $z_n \in \mathcal{Z} = \mathbb{R}^M$, $M \in \mathbb{N}$, labels $y_n \in \{ -1, +1 \}$, and weights $w_n = 1/N$, a discriminative probability distribution estimator $L : \mathbf{T} \rightarrow \{ f : \mathcal{Z} \rightarrow (0, 1) \text{ with } f(z) = p(y = +1|z) \}$, and the number of weak classifiers $T \in \mathbb{N}$

Output: strong classifier $H : \mathcal{Z} \rightarrow \mathbb{R}$ with $H(z) = \sum_{t=1}^{T} h_t(z)$

begin

  for $t = 1, \ldots, T$ **do**

    // Build probability estimator

    $f_t \leftarrow L[\mathcal{T}]$;

    $\forall_z h_t(\mathbf{Z}) \leftarrow 0.5 \cdot \log \frac{f_t(z)}{1 - f_t(z)}$;

    // Adapt sample weights

    for $n = 1, \ldots, N$ **do**

      $\mid$ $w_n \leftarrow w_n \cdot \exp\left(-y_n h_t(z)\right)$;

    end

    for $n = 1, \ldots, N$ **do**

      $\mid$ $w_n \leftarrow w_n / (\sum_{n=1}^{N} w_n)$;

    end

  end

  return $H(z) = \sum_{t=1}^{T} h_t(z)$;

end

Appendix B

Segmentation Accuracy Assessment

In this appendix, we formally introduce the measures used to assess the quality of automatically generated segmentation results. They can be grouped into two classes: First, the ones considering individual voxels and the labels assigned to them. We will refer to them as mask-based segmentation accuracy measures. Second, the ones taking into account the shape of structures that were about to be detected. They quantify match or mismatch between automatically segmented shapes and their counterparts defined in the ground-truth annotations. Accordingly, they are referred to as shape-based segmentation accuracy measures. Gerig et al. [45] and Niessen et al. [79] give a more detailed overview of various accuracy measures and their characteristics.

B.1 Mask-Based Segmentation Accuracy Measures

Let $\mathcal{S} = \{1, \dots, N\}$, $N \in \mathbb{N}$, be a set of indices to image voxels and let $\boldsymbol{x} = (x_s)_{s \in \mathcal{S}}$ and $\boldsymbol{y} = (y_s)_{s \in \mathcal{S}}$ be labelings of a given image in terms of $K \in \mathbb{N}$ possible voxel labels where $x_s, y_s \in \mathcal{X} = \{1, \dots, K\}$ for all $s \in \mathcal{S}$—in short $\boldsymbol{x}, \boldsymbol{y} \in \mathcal{X}^N$. The former, $\boldsymbol{x}$, can be thought of as a labeling, i.e., segmentation in our nomenclature, produced by a automatic or semi-automatic system, and the latter, $\boldsymbol{y}$, as a ground-truth labeling of a medical image at hand.

The number of true positives with respect to a certain label is defined as

$$TP(\boldsymbol{x}, \boldsymbol{y}, k) = |\{\, s \in \mathcal{S} | x_s = k, y_s = k \,\}|. \tag{B.1}$$

Analoguously, we have

$$FP(\boldsymbol{x}, \boldsymbol{y}, k) = |\{\, s \in \mathcal{S} | x_s = k, y_s \neq k \,\}| \tag{B.2}$$

for the number of false positives,

$$FN(\boldsymbol{x}, \boldsymbol{y}, k) = |\{\, s \in \mathcal{S} | x_s \neq k, y_s = k \,\}| \tag{B.3}$$

for the number of false negatives, and

$$TN(\boldsymbol{x}, \boldsymbol{y}, k) = |\{\, s \in \mathcal{S} | x_s \neq k, y_s \neq k \,\}| \tag{B.4}$$

for the number of true negatives.

The Dice coefficient (Dice coeff.) [31], measuring similarity between the ground-truth and a segmentation result with respect to a certain label, is defined as

$$D(\boldsymbol{x}, \boldsymbol{y}, k) = \frac{2 \cdot TP(\boldsymbol{x}, \boldsymbol{y}, k)}{FP(\boldsymbol{x}, \boldsymbol{y}, k) + 2 \cdot TP(\boldsymbol{x}, \boldsymbol{y}, k) + FN(\boldsymbol{x}, \boldsymbol{y}, k)}. \tag{B.5}$$

Similarily, the Jaccard coefficient (Jaccard coeff.) [105] is defined as

$$J(\boldsymbol{x}, \boldsymbol{y}, k) = \frac{TP(\boldsymbol{x}, \boldsymbol{y}, k)}{FP(\boldsymbol{x}, \boldsymbol{y}, k) + TP(\boldsymbol{x}, \boldsymbol{y}, k) + FN(\boldsymbol{x}, \boldsymbol{y}, k)}. \tag{B.6}$$

It gives raise to the volumetric overlap error (overlap err.) [56], which is defined as

$$VOE(\boldsymbol{x}, \boldsymbol{y}, k) = 1 - J(\boldsymbol{x}, \boldsymbol{y}, k). \tag{B.7}$$

The relative absolute volume difference (volume diff.) is defined by

$$VD(\boldsymbol{x}, \boldsymbol{y}, k) = \frac{|\{\, s \in \mathcal{S} | x_s = k \,\}| - |\{\, s \in \mathcal{S} | y_s = k \,\}|}{|\{\, s \in \mathcal{S} | y_s = k \,\}|}. \tag{B.8}$$

For the Pearson correlation coefficient [35] the two sets of components of $\boldsymbol{x}$ and $\boldsymbol{y}$ are interpreted as random samples of two discrete random variables X and Y. The correlation coefficient is then defined as

$$\rho = \frac{\sigma_{XY}}{\sigma_X \sigma_Y} \tag{B.9}$$

where σ_{XY} is the covariance of X and Y, and σ_X and σ_Y are the standard deviations of X and Y, respectively.

B.2   Shape-Based Segmentation Accuracy Measures

The calculation of shape based accuracy measures is typically not straightforward when no point to point correspondences of the shape representation are available. [45] In the "3-D Segmentation in the Clinic: A Grand Challenge" competition [1] [56] the base representa-

---

[1]www.cause07.org

tion of segmentation results and ground-truth annotations is chosen to be mask images. Accordingly, informal descriptions on how to compute the measures are provided [56]:

For the average symmetric absolute surface distance (abs. dist.), the border voxels of the segmentation result and the ground-truth annotation are determined. They are defined as those voxels of the structure having at least one neighbor, of their 18 nearest neighbors, that does not belong to the structure. For each border voxel of the segmentation result the closest voxel on the border of the ground-truth annotation is found out. This is done using Euclidean distance in physical space, that is, anisotropic voxel spacing is taken into account. The average of all these distances both from the segmentation result to the ground-truth annotation as well as vice versa gives the average symmetric absolute surface distance. The root mean square symmetric absolute surface distance (RMS dist.) is similar to the previous one. It stores the squared distances between the two sets of border voxels instead of the plain Euclidean distances. Afterwards these values are averaged and the square root is extracted. The maximum symmetric absolute surface distance (max. dist.) differs from both the previous measures in that the maximum of all voxel distances is taken instead of the average.

Appendix C

Procrustes Analysis

C.1 Ordinary Procrustes Analysis

The purpose of ordinary Procrustes analysis (OPA) is the matching of two shapes $x, y \in \mathbb{R}^{nm}$ of $n \in \mathbb{N}^+$ control points of dimension $m \in \mathbb{N}^+$ with similarity transformations using least square techniques. As we deal with 3-D objects and shapes we restrict our considerations to $m = 3$. References [103] and [34] give a more detailed representation of the results we are going to present here. They also consider the more general case.

By carrying out a full OPA we want to solve for

$$
\begin{aligned}
(\hat{s}, \hat{R}, \hat{t}) \;\; = \;\; & \arg\min_{s, R, t} O(x, y) \\
= \;\; & \arg\min_{s, R, t} \| y - M(s, R, t)[x] \|^2
\end{aligned}
\tag{C.1}
$$

where $\| x \| = (\sum_{i=1}^{n} x_{i_1}^2 + x_{i_2}^2 + x_{i_3}^2)^{\frac{1}{2}}$ is the Euclidean norm in $\mathbb{R}^{n3}$. The operator $M(s, R, t) : \mathbb{R}^{n3} \rightarrow \mathbb{R}^{n3}$ applies the affine transformation associated with scaling factor $s \in \mathbb{R}$, orientation $R \in \mathcal{SO}(3)$ (3-D rotation group), and translation $t \in \mathbb{R}^3$ to all points $(x_{i_1}, x_{i_2}, x_{i_3})^T$, $i \in \{1, \ldots, n\}$, of shape x. The function $O : \mathbb{R}^{n3} \times \mathbb{R}^{n3} \rightarrow \mathbb{R}$ is called ordinary (Procrustes) sum of squares.

Let $c_1 = \frac{1}{n} \sum_{i=1}^{n} (x_{i_1}, x_{i_2}, x_{i_3})^T$ and $c_2 = \frac{1}{n} \sum_{i=1}^{n} (y_{i_1}, y_{i_2}, y_{i_3})^T$ the centers of gravity of shape x and shape y, respectively. Let further $\tilde{x} = M(1, 1, -c_1)[x]$ and $\tilde{y} = M(1, 1, -c_2)[y]$ be the zero mean versions of x and y where $1 \in \mathcal{SO}(3)$ is the neutral element of the 3-D rotation group $\mathcal{SO}(3)$. Following the representation in reference [103] a solution to Equation (C.1) is given by $(\hat{s}, \hat{\boldsymbol{R}}, \hat{\boldsymbol{t}})$ with translation $\hat{\boldsymbol{t}} = \boldsymbol{c}_1 - \boldsymbol{c}_2$, orientation $\hat{\boldsymbol{R}} = \boldsymbol{U}\boldsymbol{V}^T$ [65] where

$$
\boldsymbol{A} = \begin{pmatrix} \tilde{y}_{1_1} & \tilde{y}_{2_1} & \cdots & \tilde{y}_{n_1} \\ \tilde{y}_{1_2} & \tilde{y}_{2_2} & \cdots & \tilde{y}_{n_2} \\ \tilde{y}_{1_3} & \tilde{y}_{2_3} & \cdots & \tilde{y}_{n_3} \end{pmatrix} \cdot \begin{pmatrix} \tilde{x}_{1_1} & \tilde{x}_{1_2} & \tilde{x}_{1_3} \\ \tilde{x}_{2_1} & \tilde{x}_{2_2} & \tilde{x}_{2_3} \\ \vdots & \vdots & \vdots \\ \tilde{x}_{n_1} & \tilde{x}_{n_2} & \tilde{x}_{n_3} \end{pmatrix} = \boldsymbol{V}\boldsymbol{\Sigma}\boldsymbol{U}^T \tag{C.2}
$$

with

$$
\boldsymbol{\Sigma} = \begin{pmatrix} \lambda_1 & 0 & 0 \\ 0 & \lambda_2 & 0 \\ 0 & 0 & \lambda_3 \end{pmatrix} \in \mathbb{R}^{3\times3}, \tag{C.3}
$$

and scaling

$$
\hat{s} = \frac{\sum_{i=1}^n \tilde{x}_{i_1}^P \tilde{y}_{i_1} + \tilde{x}_{i_2}^P \tilde{y}_{i_2} + \tilde{x}_{i_3}^P \tilde{y}_{i_3}}{\sum_{i=1}^n \tilde{x}_{i_1}^2 + \tilde{x}_{i_2}^2 + \tilde{x}_{i_3}^2} \tag{C.4}
$$

where $\tilde{\boldsymbol{x}}^P = M(1, \hat{\boldsymbol{R}}, 0)[\tilde{\boldsymbol{x}}]$. Equation (C.2) involves a singular value decomposition (SVD) of both the shapes' covariance matrix, which can be solved for through fast numerical algorithms [89].

C.2   Generalized Procrustes Anaylsis

While full OPA serves to match one shape to another, the problem of finding a population mean shape $\bar{x}$ of two and more shapes is addressed by full generalized Procrustes analysis (GPA) [51], which is a direct generalization of OPA. We describe GPA in accordance with Dryden and Mardia [34] in the following. The approach is motivated by the perturbation model

$$
\boldsymbol{x}_i = M(s_i, \boldsymbol{R}_i, \boldsymbol{t}_i)[\bar{\boldsymbol{x}} + \boldsymbol{e}_i], \tag{C.5}
$$

$i \in \{1, \ldots, N\}, N \in \mathbb{N}^+\backslash\{1\}$, for a population of shapes $\boldsymbol{x}_i \in \mathbb{R}^{n3}, n \in \mathbb{N}^+$, where $\boldsymbol{e}_i \in \mathbb{R}^{n3}$ are zero mean independent random error vectors. In cases where the shapes are commensurate in scale the perturbation model is

$$
\boldsymbol{x}_i = M(1, \boldsymbol{R}_i, \boldsymbol{t}_i)[\bar{\boldsymbol{x}} + \boldsymbol{e}_i]. \tag{C.6}
$$

Methodically, GPA is an ordinary least squares approach to finding an estimate of $\bar{x}$. For that, the objective function

$$
\begin{aligned}
(\hat{s}_i, \hat{\boldsymbol{R}}_i, \hat{\boldsymbol{t}}_i)_{i=1,\dots,N} &= \arg\min_{(s_i, \boldsymbol{R}_i, \boldsymbol{t}_i)_i} G(\boldsymbol{x}_1, \boldsymbol{x}_2, \dots, \boldsymbol{x}_N) \\
&= \arg\min_{(s_i, \boldsymbol{R}_i, \boldsymbol{t}_i)_i} \frac{1}{N} \sum_{i=1}^{N} \sum_{j=i+1}^{N} \| M(s_i, \boldsymbol{R}_i, \boldsymbol{t}_i)[\boldsymbol{x}_i] - M(s_j, \boldsymbol{R}_j, \boldsymbol{t}_j)[\boldsymbol{x}_j] \|^2
\end{aligned}
\tag{C.7}
$$

is minimized subject to a constraint on the centroid size of the average, that is to say,

$$
\left(\sum_{i=1}^{n} \sum_{j=1}^{3} (\bar{x}_{ij} - \bar{c}_j)^2 \right)^{\frac{1}{2}} = 1
\tag{C.8}
$$

where $\bar{c} = (\bar{c}_1, \bar{c}_2, \bar{c}_3)^T$ is the centroid of $\bar{x}$. The average configuration is

$$
\bar{x} = \sum_{i=1}^{n} M(\hat{s}_i, \hat{\boldsymbol{R}}_i, \hat{\boldsymbol{t}}_i)[\boldsymbol{x}_i].
\tag{C.9}
$$

The function $G : (\mathbb{R}^{n3})^N \to \mathbb{R}$ is called generalized (Procrustes) sum of squares.

Algorithm 7 serves to estimate the "nuisance parameters" [34, 49] $(\hat{s}_i, \hat{\boldsymbol{R}}_i, \hat{\boldsymbol{t}}_i)$, $i \in \{1, \dots, N\}$. Once they are found the full Procrustes coordinates of each of the $\boldsymbol{x}_i$, $i \in \{1, \dots, N\}$, are given by

$$
\boldsymbol{x}_i^P = M(\hat{s}_i, \hat{\boldsymbol{R}}_i, \hat{\boldsymbol{t}}_i)[\boldsymbol{x}_i].
\tag{C.10}
$$

In accordance with Equation (C.6), the removal of scaling, that is, step 3 in Algorithm 7, can be omitted. [51]

In general, it may be possible to find more realistic estimates of $\bar{x}$ by a total least squares approach where the perturbation model additionally takes into account variations of the shapes' surface sampling points. A detailed analysis of this is out of scope of this appendix.

Algorithm 7: GPA algorithm [34]

Input: population of shapes $x_i \in \mathbb{R}^{n3}$, $n \in \mathbb{N}^+$, $i \in \{1, \dots, N\}$, $N \in \mathbb{N}^+ \backslash \{1\}$

Output: population of shapes $x_i^P \in \mathbb{R}^{n3}$, $i \in \{1, \dots, N\}$, aligned in model space, nuisance
   parameters $(\hat{s}_i, \hat{R}_i, \hat{t}_i)$, $i \in \{1, \dots, N\}$

begin

   // 1. Remove translations

   forall $i \in \{1, \dots, N\}$ **do**

      // Compute centroid c_i of shape x_i

      $\hat{t}_i = -c_i$;

      $x_i^P = M(1, 1, t_i)[x_i]$;

   end

   $\Delta G = +\infty$;

   repeat

      // 2. Remove rotations

      repeat

         forall $i \in \{1, \dots, N\}$ **do**

            $\bar{x}_i = \frac{1}{N-1} \sum_{j \neq i} x_j^P$;

            $(\hat{s}_i, \hat{R}_i, \hat{t}_i) = \arg\min_{s, R, t} O(x_i^P, \bar{x}_i)$;

            $\hat{x}_i^P = M(1, \hat{R}_i, 0)[x_i^P]$;

         end

         $\Delta G = |G(x_1^P, x_2^P, \dots, x_N^P) - G(\hat{x}_1^P, \hat{x}_2^P, \dots, \hat{x}_N^P)|$;

         forall $i \in \{1, \dots, N\}$ **do**

            $x_i^P = \hat{x}_i^P$;

         end

      until $\Delta G < \epsilon$ *for some* $\epsilon > 0$;

      // 3. Remove scaling

      // a) Compute correlation matrix

      $C = \left(\text{corr}(\hat{x}_i^P, \hat{x}_j^P) \right)_{i=1,\dots,N, j=1,\dots,N}$;

      // b) Compute eigenvector corresponding to largest eigenvalue of correlation matrix

      $v = (v_1, \dots, v_N)^T$;

      // c) Update scaling parameters

      forall $i \in \{1, \dots, N\}$ **do**

         $\hat{s}_i = \left(\frac{\sum_{k=1}^{N} \|x_k^P\|^2}{\|x_i^P\|^2} \right)^{\frac{1}{2}} v_i$ [8];

         $\hat{x}_i^P = M(\hat{s}_i, 1, 0)[\hat{x}_i^P]$;

      end

      $\Delta G = |G(x_1^P, x_2^P, \dots, x_N^P) - G(\hat{x}_1^P, \hat{x}_2^P, \dots, \hat{x}_N^P)|$;

      forall $i \in \{1, \dots, N\}$ **do**

         $x_i^P = \hat{x}_i^P$;

      end

   until $\Delta G < \epsilon$ *for some* $\epsilon > 0$;

end

Appendix D

Acronyms and Abbreviations

1-D	one-dimensional
2-D	two-dimensional
3-D	three-dimensional
abs. dist.	(average symmetric) absolute (surface) distance
ASM	active shape model
BET	Brain Extraction Tool
CAD	computer-aided diagnosis
CNS	central nervous system
COV	coefficient of variation
CSF	cerebral spinal fluid
CT	computed tomography
DHW	dynamic histogram warping
Dice coeff.	Dice coefficient
DMC-EM	discriminative model-constrained HMRF EM
DMC-GC	discriminative model-constrained graph cuts
DTW	dynamic time warping
EM	expectation maximization
EMD	earth mover's distance
FAST	FMRIB's Automated Segmentation Tool
FGM	finite Gaussian mixture
FLIRT	FMRIB's Linear Registration Tool
FN	false negatives
FP	false positives
GM	(cerebral) gray matter
GPA	generalized Procrustes analysis
HMC	hidden Markov chains
HMRF	hidden Markov random field

HMRF-EM	hidden Markov random field expectation maximization
HUM	homomorphic unsharp masking
i.i.d.	independently and identically distributed
IBSR	Internet Brain Segmentation Repository
ICM	iterated conditional modes
INU	intensity non-uniformity
Jaccard coeff.	Jaccard coefficient
MAP	maximum a posteriori
max. dist.	maximum (symmetric absolute surface) distance
MICCAI	medical image computing and computer-assisted intervention
MPM	maximizer of the posterior marginals
MR	magnetic resonance
MRF	Markov random field
MRI	magnetic resonance imaging
MRT	magnetic resonance tomography
MSL	marginal space learning
N3	nonparametric nonuniform intensity normalization
NMR	nuclear magnetic resonance
OPA	ordinary Procrustes analysis
overlap err.	(volumetric) overlap error
PBT	probabilistic boosting-tree
PCA	principal component analysis
PD	proton density
PDF	probability density function
PDM	point distribution model
PVE	partial volume effect
RAI	right-to-left, anterior-to-posterior, inferior-to-superior
RF	radio frequency
RMS dist.	root mean square (symmetric absolute surface) distance
SVD	singular value decomposition
TN	true negatives
TP	true positives
US	ultrasound
volume diff.	(relative absolute) volume difference
WM	(cerebral) white matter

Bibliography

[1] A. Akselrod-Ballin, M. Galun, J. M. Gomori, R. Basri, and A. Brandt. Atlas guided identification of brain structures by combining 3D segmentation and SVM classification. In R. Larsen, M. Nielsen, and J. Sporring, editors, *Int. Conf. Med. Image Comput. Comput.-Assist. Interv., Copenhagen, Denmark*, pages 209–216, Oct. 2006.

[2] A. Akselrod-Ballin, M. Galun, J. M. Gomori, A. Brandt, and R. Basri. Prior knowledge driven multiscale segmentation of brain MRI. In N. Ayache, S. Ourselin, and A. Maeder, editors, *Int. Conf. Med. Image Comput. Comput.-Assist. Interv., Brisbane, Australia*, pages 118–126, Oct. 2007.

[3] E. Anger, editor. *Meyers Taschenlexikon: In 10 Bänden*. BI-Taschenbuchverl., Mannheim, 1992.

[4] J. Ashburner and K. J. Friston. Unified segmentation. *NeuroImage*, 26(3):839–851, Apr. 2005.

[5] S. P. Awate, T. Tasdizen, N. Foster, and R. T. Whitaker. Adaptive Markov modeling for mutual-information-based, unsupervised MRI brain-tissue classification. *Med. Image Anal.*, 10(5):726–739, Oct. 2006.

[6] P.-L. Bazin and D. L. Pham. Homeomorphic brain image segmentation with topological and statistical atlases. *Med. Image Anal.*, 12(5):616–625, Oct. 2008.

[7] B. Belaroussi, J. Milles, S. Carme, Y. M. Zhu, and H. Benoit-Cattin. Intensity non-uniformity correction in MRI: existing methods and their validation. *Med. Image Anal.*, 10(2):234–246, Apr. 2006.

[8] J. M. F. Ten Berge. Orthogonal procrustes rotation for two or more matrices. *Psychometrika*, 42:267–276, 1977.

[9] J. Besag. On the statistical analysis of dirty pictures. *J. Roy. Stat. Soc. B Stat. Meth.*, 48(3):259–302, 1986.

[10] Y. Boykov and G. Funka-Lea. Graph cuts and efficient N-D image segmentation. *Int. J. Comput. Vis.*, 70(2):109–131, Nov. 2006.

[11] Y. Boykov and V. Kolmogorov. An experimental comparison of min-cut/max-flow algorithms for energy minimization in vision. *IEEE Trans. Pattern Anal. Mach. Intell.*, 26(9):1124–1137, Sept. 2004.

[12] L. Breiman. Random forests. *Mach. Learn.*, 45(1):5–32, Oct. 2001.

[13] S. Bricq, Ch. Collet, and J. P. Armspach. Unifying framework for multimodal brain MRI segmentation based on hidden Markov chains. *Med. Image Anal.*, 12(6):639–652, Dec. 2008.

[14] B. H. Brinkmann, A. Manduca, and R. A. Robb. Optimized homomorphic unsharp masking for MR grayscale inhomogeneity correction. *IEEE Trans. Med. Imag.*, 17(2):161–171, Apr. 1998.

[15] M. A. Brown and R. C. Semelka. *MRI: Basic Principles and Applications*. John Wiles & Sons, Inc., Hoboken, NJ, USA, 3 edition, 2003.

[16] E. Bullitt, D. Zeng, G. Gerig, S Aylward, S. Joshi, J. K. Smith, W. Lin, and M. G. Ewend. Vessel tortuosity and brain tumor malignancy: A blinded study. *Acad. Radiol.*, 12(10):1232–1240, Oct. 2005.

[17] G. Carneiro, F. Amat, B. Georgescu, S. Good, and D. Comaniciu. Semantic-based indexing of fetal anatomies from 3-D ultrasound data using global/semi-local context and sequential sampling. In *IEEE Comput. Soc. Conf. Comput. Vis. Pattern Recogn., Achorage, AK, USA*, June 2008.

[18] G. Carneiro, B. Georgescu, S. Good, and D. Comaniciu. Automatic fetal measurements in ultrasound using constrained probabilistic boosting tree. In *Int. Conf. Med. Image Comput. Comput.-Assist. Interv., Brisbane, Australia*, Oct. 2007.

[19] G. Carneiro, B. Georgescu, S. Good, and D. Comaniciu. Detection and measurement of fetal anatomies from ultrasound images using a constrained probabilistic boosting tree. *IEEE Trans. Med. Imag.*, 27(9):1342–1355, Sept. 2008.

[20] M. Chupin, A. Hammers, E. Bardinet, O. Colliot, R. S. N. Liu, J. S. Duncan, L. Garnero, and L. Lemieux. Fully automatic segmentation of the hippocampus and the amygdala from MRI using hybrid prior knowledge. In *Int. Conf. Med. Image Comput. Comput.-Assist. Interv., Brisbane, Australia*, pages 875–882, Oct. 2007.

[21] D. Cobzas, N. Birkbeck, M. Schmidt, M. Jagersand, and A. Murtha. 3D variational brain tumor segmentation using a high dimensional feature set. In *Proceedings of the Mathematical Methods in Biomedical Image Analysis (MMBIA) Workshop, Rio de Janeiro, Brazil*, Oct. 2007.

[22] C. A. Cocosco, V. Kollokian, R. K.-S. Kwan, and A. C. Evans. BrainWeb: Online interface to a 3D MRI simulated brain database. In *Int. Conf. Func. Mapp. Hum. Brain, Copenhagen, Denmark*, page 425, May 1997.

[23] T. F. Cootes, A. Hill, C. J. Taylor, and J. Haslam. The use of active shape models for locating structures in medical images. *Image Vis. Comput.*, 12(6):355–366, Jul. 1994.

[24] T. F. Cootes, C. J. Taylor, D. H. Cooper, and J. Graham. Active shape models—their training and application. *Comput. Vis. Image Understand.*, 61(1):38–59, Jan. 1995.

[25] J. J. Corso, E. Sharon, S. Dube, S. El-Saden, U. Sinha, and A. Yuille. Efficient multilevel brain tumor segmentation with integrated Bayesian model classification. *IEEE Trans. Med. Imag.*, 27(5):629–640, May 2008.

[26] J. J. Corso, E. Sharon, and A. L. Yuille. Multilevel segmentation and integrated Bayesian model classification with an application to brain tumor segmentation. In *Int. Conf. Med. Image Comput. Comput.-Assist. Interv., Copenhagen, Denmark*, pages 790–798, Oct. 2006.

[27] J. J. Corso, Z. Tu, A. Yuille, and A. Toga. Segmentation of sub-cortical structures by the graph-shifts algorithm. In *Int. Conf. Inform. Process. Med. Imag., Kerkrade, the Netherlands*, pages 183–197, July 2007.

[28] J. J. Corso, A. Yuille, N. L. Sicotte, and A. Toga. Detection and segmentation of pathological structures by the extended graph-shifts algorithm. In *Int. Conf. Med. Image Comput. Comput.-Assist. Interv., Brisbane, Australia*, pages 985–993, Oct. 2007.

[29] I. J. Cox and S. L. Hingorani. Dynamic histogram warping of image pairs for constant image brightness. In *Int. Conf. Image Process., Vol. II, Washington, D.C., USA*, pages 366–369, Oct. 1995.

[30] M. Bach Cuadra, L. Cammoun, T. Butz, O. Cuisenaire, and J.-P. Thiran. Comparison and validation of tissue modelization and statistical classification methods in T1-weighted MR brain images. *IEEE Trans. Med. Imag.*, 24(12):1548–1565, Dec. 2005.

[31] L. R. Dice. Measures of the amount of ecologic association between species. *Ecology*, 26(3):297–302, July 1945.

[32] E. A. Dinic. Algorithm for solution of a problem of maximum flow in a network with power estimation. *Soviet Math. Dokl.*, 11(5):1277–1280, 1970.

[33] R. L. Drake, W. Vogl, and A. W. M. Mitchell. *Gray's Anatomy for Students*. Elsevier/Churchill Livingstone, Philadelphia, PA, USA, London, UK, 2005.

[34] I. L. Dryden and K. V. Mardia. *Statistical Shape Analysis*. John Wiley & Sons, Chichester, West Sussex, England, 1998.

[35] R. O. Duda, P. E. Hart, and D. G. Stork. *Pattern Classification*. John Wiley & Sons, 2 edition, 2001.

[36] J. Edmonds and R. M. Karp. Theoretical improvements in algorithmic efficiency for network flow problems. *J. ACM*, 19(2):248–264, Apr. 1972.

[37] B. Fischl, D. H. Salat, E. Busa, M. Albert, M. Dieterich, C. Haselgrove, A. van der Kouwe, R. Killiany, D. Kennedy, S. Klaveness, A. Montillo, N. Makris, B. Rosen, and A. M. Dale. Whole brain segmentation: Automated labeling of neuroanatomical structures in the human brain. *Neuron*, 33(3):341–355, Jan. 2002.

[38] B. Fischl, D. H. Salat, A. J. van der Kouwe, N. Makris, F. Ségonne, B. T. Quinn, and A. M. Dale. Sequence-independent segmentation of magnetic resonance images. *NeuroImage*, 23(1):69–84, Sept. 2004.

[39] L.M. Fletcher-Heath, L. O. Hall, D. B. Goldgof, and F. R. Murtagh. Automatic segmentation of non-enhancing brain tumors in magnetic resonance images. *Artif. Intell. Med.*, 21(1–3):43–63, 2001.

[40] L. R. Ford and D. R. Fulkerson. Maximal flow through a network. *Can. J. Math.*, 8:399–404, 1956.

[41] Y. Freund and R. E. Schapire. A decision-theoretic generalization of on-line learning and an application to boosting. In *Europ. Conf. Comput. Learn. Theor.*, pages 23–37, Mar. 1995.

[42] J. Friedman, T. Hastie, and R. Tibshirani. Additive logistic regression: a statistical view of boosting. *Ann. Stat.*, 28(2):337–407, Apr. 2000.

[43] Y. Ge, J. K. Udupa, L. G. Nyúl, L. Wei, and R. I. Grossman. Numerical tissue characterization in MS via standardization of the MR image intensity scale. *J. Magn. Reson. Imag.*, 12(5):715–721, 2000.

[44] B. Georgescu, X. S. Zhou, D. Comaniciu, and A. Gupta. Database-guided segmentation of anatomical structures with complex appearance. In *IEEE Comput. Soc. Conf. Comput. Vis. Pattern Recogn., San Diego, CA, USA*, June 2005.

[45] G. Gerig, M. Jomier, and M. Chakos. Valmet: A new validation tool for assessing and improving 3D object segmentation. In *Int. Conf. Med. Image Comput. Comput.-Assist. Interv., Utrecht, The Netherlands*, pages 516–523, Oct. 2001.

[46] D. T. Gering, W. E. L. Grimson, and R. Kikinis. Recognizing deviations from normalcy for brain tumor segmentation. In *Int. Conf. Med. Image Comput. Comput.-Assist. Interv., Tokyo, Japan*, pages 388–395, Sept. 2002.

[47] P. Gibbs, D. L. Buckley, S. J. Blackband, and A. Horsman. Tumour volume determination from MR images by morphological segmentation. *Phys. Med. Biol.*, 41(11):2437–2446, 1996.

[48] A. V. Goldberg and R. E. Tarjan. A new approach to the maximum-flow problem. *J. ACM*, 35(4):921–940, Oct. 1988.

[49] C. R. Goodall and K. V. Mardia. A geometrical derivation of the shape density. *Adv. Appl. Probab.*, 23:496–514, 1992.

[50] S. Gouttard, M. Styner, S. Joshi, R. G. Smith, H. Cody, and G. Gerig. Subcortical structure segmentation using probabilistic atlas priors. In *SPIE Med. Imag.: Image Process., San Diego, CA, USA*, volume 6512, pages 65122J–1–11, Feb. 2007.

[51] J. C. Gower. Generalized Procrustes analysis. *Psychometrika*, 40(1):33–50, Mar. 1975.

[52] D. Greig, B. Porteous, and A. Seheult. Exact maximum a posteriori estimation for binary images. *J. Roy. Stat. Soc. B Stat. Meth.*, 51(2):271–279, 1989.

[53] R. Guillemaud and J. M. Brady. Estimating the bias field of MR images. *IEEE Trans. Med. Imag.*, 16(3):238–251, June 1997.

[54] X. Han and B. Fischl. Atlas renormalization for improved brain MR image segmentation across scanner platforms. *IEEE Trans. Med. Imag.*, 26(4):479–486, Apr. 2007.

[55] R. A. Heckemann, J. V. Hajnal, P. Aljabar, D. Rueckert, and A. Hammers. Automatic anatomical brain MRI segmentation combining label propagation and decision fusion. *NeuroImage*, 33(1):115–126, Oct. 2006.

[56] T. Heimann, M. Styner, and B. van Ginneken. Workshop on 3D segmentation in the clinic: A grand challenge. In: T. Heimann, M. Styner, B. van Ginneken (Eds.): 3D Segmentation in the Clinic: A Grand Challenge, Oct. 2007. 7–15.

[57] S. Ho, E. Bullitt, and G. Gerig. Level set evolution with region competition: Automatic 3-D segmentation of brain tumors. In *Int. Conf. Pattern Recogn., Quebec, Canada*, pages 532–535, Aug. 2002.

[58] K. M. Iftekharuddin, M. A. Islam, J. Shaik, C. Parra, and R. Ogg. Automatic brain tumor detection in MRI: Methodology and statistical validation. In *SPIE Med. Imag.: Image Process., Bellingham, WA, USA*, volume 5747, pages 2012–2022, 2005.

[59] R. I. Ionasec, B. Georgescu, E. Gassner, S. Vogt, O. Kutter, M. Scheuering, N. Navab, and D. Comaniciu. Dynamic model-driven quantitative and visual evaluation of the aortic valve from 4D CT. In *Int. Conf. Med. Image Comput. Comput.-Assist. Interv., New York, NY, USA*, pages 686–694, Sept. 2008.

[60] F. Jäger and J. Hornegger. Nonrigid registration of joint histograms for intensity standardization in magnetic resonance imaging. *IEEE Trans. Med. Imag.*, 28(1):137–150, Jan. 2009.

[61] M. Jenkinson and S. M. Smith. A global optimisation method for robust affine registration of brain images. *Med. Image Anal.*, 5(2):143–156, June 2001.

[62] T. Kapur, W. E. L. Grimson, R. Kikinis, and W. M. Wells. Enhanced spatial priors for segmentation of magnetic resonance imagery. In *Int. Conf. Med. Image Comput. Comput.-Assist. Interv.*, Cambridge, MA, USA, pages 457–468, Oct. 1998.

[63] M. R. Kaus, S. K. Warfield, A. Nabavi, P. M. Black, F. A. Jolesz, and R. Kikinis. Automated segmentation of MR images of brain tumors. *Radiology*, 218:586–591, 2001.

[64] M. R. Kaus, S. K. Warfield, A. Nabavi, E. Chatzidakis, P. M. Black, F. A. Jolesz, and R. Kikinis. Segmentation of meningiomas and low grade gliomas in MRI. In *Int. Conf. Med. Image Comput. Comput.-Assist. Interv.*, Cambridge, UK, pages 1–10, Sept. 1999.

[65] D. G. Kendall. Shape manifolds, procrustean metrics, and complex projective spaces. *Bull. London Math. Soc.*, 16(2):81–121, 1984.

[66] J. B. Kruskal and M. Liberman. *Time Warps, String Edits, and Macromolecules: The Theory and Practice of Sequence Comparison*, chapter The Symmetric Time-Warping Problem: From Continuous to Discrete, pages 125–161. Addison Wesley, Reading, MA, USA, 1983.

[67] S. Kullback and R. A. Leibler. On information and sufficiency. *Ann. Math. Stat.*, 22(1):79–86, 1951.

[68] T. Laubenberger and J. Laubenberger. *Technik der medizinischen Radiologie: Diagnostik, Strahlentherapie, Strahlenschutz für Ärzte, Medizinstudenten und MTRA*. Dt. Aerzte-Verl., Cologne, Germany, 7 edition, 1999.

[69] S. Z. Li. *Markov Random Field Modeling in Image Analysis*. Computer Sience Workbench. Springer-Verlag Tokio, Japan, July 2001.

[70] R. Lienhart, A. Kuranov, and V. Pisarevsky. Empirical analysis of detection cascades of boosted classifiers for rapid object detection. In *DAGM-Symposium*, pages 297–304, Sept. 2003.

[71] H. Ling, S. K. Zhou, Y. Zheng, B. Georgescu, M. Suehling, and D. Comaniciu. Hierarchical, learning-based automatic liver segmentation. In *IEEE Comput. Soc. Conf. Comput. Vis. Pattern Recogn.*, Brisbane, Achorage, AK, USA, June 2008.

[72] W. E. Lorensen and H. E. Cline. Marching cubes: A high resolution 3D surface construction algorithm. *Comput. Graph.*, 21(4):163–169, July 1987.

[73] L. Lu, A. Barbu, M. Wolf, J. Liang, M. Salganicoff, and D. Comaniciu. Accurate polyp segmentation for 3D CT colongraphy using multi-staged probabilistic binary learning and compositional model. In *IEEE Comput. Soc. Conf. Comput. Vis. Pattern Recogn., Anchorage, AK, USA.*, July 2008.

[74] J. L. Marroquin, B. C. Vemuri, S. Botello, F. Calderon, and A. Fernandez-Bouzas. An accurate and efficient Bayesian method for automatic segmentation of brain MRI. *IEEE Trans. Med. Imag.*, 21(8):934–945, Aug. 2002.

[75] N. Moon, E. Bullitt, K. van Leemput, and G. Gerig. Automatic brain and tumor segmentation. In *Int. Conf. Med. Image Comput. Comput.-Assist. Interv., Tokyo, Japan*, pages 372–379, Sept. 2002.

[76] N. Moon, E. Bullitt, K. van Leemput, and G. Gerig. Model-based brain and tumor segmentation. In *Int. Conf. Pattern Recogn., Quebec, Canada*, pages 528–531, Aug. 2002.

[77] J. H. Morra, Z. Tu, L. G. Apostolova, A. E. Green, A. W. Toga, and P. M. Thompson. Automatic subcortical segmentation using a contextual model. In *Int. Conf. Med. Image Comput. Comput.-Assist. Interv., New York, NY, USA*, pages 194–201, Sept. 2008.

[78] M. Murgasova, L. Dyet, A. D. Edwards, M. A. Rutherford, J. V. Hajnal, and D. Rueckert. Segmentation of brain MRI in young children. In *Int. Conf. Med. Image Comput. Comput.-Assist. Interv., Copenhagen, Denmark*, pages 687–694, Oct. 2006.

[79] W. J. Niessen, C. J. Bouma, K. L. Vincken, and M. A. Viergever. Error metrics for quantitative evaluation of medical image segmentation. In R. Klette, H. S. Stiehl, M. A. Viergever, and K. L. Vincken, editors, *Perform. Char. Comput. Vis.*, Computational Imaging and Vision, Dordrecht, 2000.

[80] R. D. Nowak. Wavelet-based Rician noise removal for magnetic resonance imaging. *IEEE Trans. Image Process.*, 8(10):1408–1419, 1999.

[81] L. G. Nyúl and J. K. Udupa. On standardizing the MR image intensity scale. *Magn. Reson. Med.*, 42:1072–1081, 1999.

[82] L. G. Nyúl, J. K. Udupa, and X. Zhang. New variants of a method of MRI scale standardization. *IEEE Trans. Med. Imag.*, 19(2):143–150, Feb. 2000.

[83] M. Oren, C. Papageorgiou, P. Sinha, E. Osuna, and T. Poggio. Pedestrian detection using wavelet templates. In *IEEE Comput. Soc. Conf. Comput. Vis. Pattern Recogn., San Juan, Puerto Rico*, pages 193–199, June 1997.

[84] D. L. Pham, C. Xu, and J. L. Prince. Current methods in medical image segmentation. *Annu. Rev. Biomed. Eng.*, 2:315–337, 2000.

[85] K. M. Pohl, J. Fisher, J. J. Levitt, M. E. Shenton, R. Kikinis, W. E. L. Grimson, and W. M. Wells. A unifying approach to registration, segmentation, and intensity correction. In *Int. Conf. Med. Image Comput. Comput.-Assist. Interv., Palm Springs, CA, USA*, pages 310–318, Oct. 2005.

[86] K. M. Pohl, W. M. Wells, A. Guimond, K. Kasai, M. E. Shenton, R. Kikinis, W. E. L. Grimson, and S. K. Warfield. Incoperating non-rigid registration into expectation maximization algorithm to segment MR images. In *Int. Conf. Med. Image Comput. Comput.-Assist. Interv., Tokyo, Japan*, pages 564–572, Sept. 2002.

[87] M. Prastawa, E. Bullitt, S. Ho, and G. Gerig. Robust estimation for brain tumor segmentation. In *Int. Conf. Med. Image Comput. Comput.-Assist. Interv., Montreal, Canada*, pages 530–537, Nov. 2003.

[88] M. Prastawa, E. Bullitt, S. Ho, and G. Gerig. A brain tumor segmentation framework based on outlier detection. *Med. Image Anal.*, 8(3):275–283, Sept. 2004.

[89] W. H. Press, S. A. Teukolsky, W. T. Vetterling, and B. P. Flannery. *Numerical Recipes in C: The Art of Scientific Computing*. Cambridge University Press, Cambridge, UK, 2 edition, 1992.

[90] J. R. Quinlan. Induction of decision trees. *Mach. Learn.*, 1(1):81–106, Mar. 1986.

[91] D. E. Rex, J. Q. Ma, and A. W. Toga. The LONI pipeline processing environment. *NeuroImage*, 19(3):1033–1048, July 2003.

[92] Y. Rubner, C. Tomasi, and L. J. Guibas. The earth mover's distance as a metric for image retrieval. *Int. J. Comput. Vis.*, 40(2):99–121, 2000.

[93] B. Scherrer, M. Dojat, F. Forbes, and C. Garbay. LOCUS: LOcal Cooperative Unified Segmentation of MRI brain scans. In *Int. Conf. Med. Image Comput. Comput.-Assist. Interv., Brisbane, Australia*, pages 219–227, Nov. 2007.

[94] B. Scherrer, F. Forbes, C. Garbay, and M. Dojat. Fully Bayesian joint model for MR brain scan and structure segmentation. In *Int. Conf. Med. Image Comput. Comput.-Assist. Interv., New York, NY, USA*, pages 1066–1074, Sept. 2008.

[95] S. Seifert, A. Barbu, S. K. Zhou, D. Liu, J. Feulner, M. Huber, M. Suehling, A. Cavallaro, and D. Comaniciu. Hierarchical parsing and semantic navigation of full body CT data. In *SPIE Med. Imag.: Image Process., Orlando, FL, USA*, volume 7259, pages 725902–1–8, Feb. 2009.

[96] S. Silbernagl and A. Despopoulos. *Taschenatlas der Physiologie*. Georg Thieme Verl., Stuttgart, Germany, New York, NY, USA, Dt. Taschenbuch-Verl., München, Germany, 4 edition, 1991.

[97] G. Slabaugh, G. Unal, T. Fang, and M. Wels. Ultrasound-specific segmentation via decorrelation and statistical region-based active contours. In *IEEE Comput. Soc. Conf. Comput. Vis. Pattern Recogn., New York, NY, USA*, pages 45–53, June 2006.

[98] G. Slabaugh, G. Unal, M. Wels, T. Fang, and B. Rao. Statistical region-based segmentation of ultrasound images. *Ultrasound Med. Biol.*, 35(5):781–795, May 2009.

[99] J. G. Sled, A. P. Zijdenbos, and A. C. Evans. A nonparametric method for automatic correction of intensity nonuniformity in MRI data. *IEEE Trans. Med. Imag.*, 17(1):87–97, Feb. 1998.

[100] S. M. Smith. Fast robust automated brain extraction. *Hum. Brain Mapp.*, 17(3):143–155, Nov. 2002.

[101] Z. Song, N. Tustison, B. Avants, and J. Gee. Adaptive graph cuts with tissue priors for brain MRI segmentation. In *IEEE Int. Symp. Biomed. Imag.: From Nano To Macro, Arlington, VA, USA*, pages 762–765, Apr. 2006.

[102] Z. Song, N. Tustison, B. Avants, and J. C. Gee. Integrated graph cuts for brain MRI segmentation. In *Int. Conf. Med. Image Comput. Comput.-Assist. Interv., Copenhagen, Denmark*, pages 831–838, Oct. 2006.

[103] M. Sonka and J. M. Fitzpatrick. *Handbook of Medical Imaging, Vol. 2: Medical Image Processing*. SPIE—The International Society of Optical Engineering, Bellingham, Washington, USA, 2004.

[104] S. Standring. *Gray's Anatomy: The Anatomical Basis of Clinical Practice*. Elsevier/Churchill Livingstone, Edinburgh, UK, 40 edition, 2008.

[105] P.-N. Tan, M. Steinbach, and V. Kumar. *Introduction to Data Mining*. Addison-Wesley, 2005.

[106] G. Taubin. A signal processing approach to fair surface design. In *Annu. Conf. Comput. Graph. (SIGGRAPH), Los Angeles, CA, USA*, pages 351–358, Aug. 1995.

[107] O. Tsang, A. Gholipour, N. Kehtarnavaz, K. Gopinath, R. Briggs, and I. Panahi. Comparison of tissue segmentation algorithms in neuroimage analysis software tools. In *Int. IEEE EMBS Conf., Vancouver, BC, Canada*, pages 3924–3928, Aug. 2008.

[108] Z. Tu. Probabilistic boosting-tree: Learning discriminative models for classification, recognition, and clustering. In *IEEE Int. Conf. Comput. Vis., Beijing, China*, pages 1589–1596, Oct. 2005.

[109] Z. Tu, K. L. Narr, P. Dollár, I. Dinov, P. M. Thompson, and A. W. Toga. Brain anatomical structure segmentation by hybrid discriminative/generative models. *IEEE Trans. Med. Imag.*, 27(4):495–508, Apr. 2008.

[110] Z. Tu, X. Zhou, D. Comaniciu, and L. Bogoni. A learning based approach for 3D segmentation and colon detagging. In *Eur. Conf. Comput. Vis., Graz, Austria*, pages 436–448, May 2006.

[111] Z. Tu, X. S. Zhou, A. Barbu, L. Bogoni, and D. Comaniciu. Probabilistic 3D polyp detection in CT images: The role of sample alignment. In *IEEE Comput. Soc. Conf. Comput. Vis. Pattern Recogn., New York, USA*, pages 1544–1551, June 2006.

[112] K. van Leemput, F. Maes, D. Vandermeulen, and P. Suetens. Automated model-based bias field correction of MR images of the brain. *IEEE Trans. Med. Imag.*, 18(10):885–896, Oct. 1999.

[113] K. van Leemput, F. Maes, D. Vandermeulen, and P. Suetens. Automated model-based tissue classification of MR images of the brain. *IEEE Trans. Med. Imag.*, 18(10):897–908, Oct. 1999.

[114] K. van Leemput, F. Maes, D. Vandermeulen, and P. Suetens. A unifying framework for partial volume segmentation of brain MR images. *IEEE Trans. Med. Imag.*, 22(1):105–119, Jan. 2003.

[115] P. Viola and M. Jones. Robust real-time object detection. In *International Workshop on Statistical Learning and Computational Theories of Vision, Vancouver, Canada*, pages 1–25, July 2001.

[116] U. Vovk, F. Pernuš, and B. Likar. A review of methods for correction of intensity inhomogeneity in MRI. *IEEE Trans. Med. Imag.*, 26(3):405–421, Mar. 2007.

[117] D. Weishaupt, V. D. Köchli, and B. Marincek. *How Does MRI Work? An Introduction to the Physics and Function of Magnetic Resonance Imaging*. Springer-Verl. Berlin Heidelberg New York, 2 edition, 2006.

[118] W. M. Wells. Efficient synthesis of Gaussian filters by cascaded uniform filters. *IEEE Trans. Pattern Anal. Mach. Intell.*, PAMI-8(2):234–239, Mar. 1986.

[119] W. M. Wells, W. E. L. Grimson, R. Kikinis, and F. A. Jolesz. Adaptive segmentation of MRI data. *IEEE Trans. Med. Imag.*, 15(4):429–442, Aug. 1996.

[120] M. Wels, G. Carneiro, A. Aplas, M. Huber, J. Hornegger, and D. Comaniciu. Discriminative model-constrained 3-D MR image segmentation. In *HSS-Cooperation Seminar: Pattern Recognition in Medical and Health Engineering, Wildbad Kreuth, Bavaria, Germany*, pages 28–29, July 2008.

[121] M. Wels, G. Carneiro, A. Aplas, M. Huber, J. Hornegger, and D. Comaniciu. A discriminative model-constrained graph cuts approach to fully automated pediatric brain tumor segmentation in 3-D MRI. In *Int. Conf. Med. Image Comput. Comput.-Assist. Interv., New York, NY, USA*, pages 67–75, Sept. 2008.

[122] M. Wels, M. Huber, and J. Hornegger. A boosting approach for multiple sclerosis lesion segmentation in multi-spectral 3D MRI. In *Russ.-Bav. Conf. Biomed. Eng., Erlangen, Germany*, pages 116–120, July 2007.

[123] M. Wels, M. Huber, and J. Hornegger. Fully automated knowledge-based segmentation of the caudate nuclei in 3D MRI. In *3D Segmentation in the Clinic: A Grand Challenge (Int. Conf. Med. Image Comput. Comput.-Assist. Interv. 2007 Workshop Proceedings), Brisbane, QLD, Australia*, pages 19–27, Oct. 2007.

[124] M. Wels, M. Huber, and J. Hornegger. Fully automated segmentation of multiple sclerosis lesions in multispectral MRI. *Pattern Recogn. Image Anal. (OGRW 2007, Ettlingen, Germany, Aug. 20–23, 2007)*, 18(2):347–350, June 2008.

[125] M. Wels, G. Staatz, A. Rossi, M. Huber, and J. Hornegger. Anisotropic hidden Markov random field modeling for unsupervised MRI brain tissue segmentation and brain tumor detection. *Int. J. Comput. Assist. Radiol. Surg. (Proceedings of the 21st International Congress and Exhibition, Berlin, Germany, June 27–30, 2007)*, 2:457, 2007. Suppl. 1.

[126] M. Wels, Y. Zheng, G. Carneiro, M. Huber, J. Hornegger, and D. Comaniciu. Fast and robust 3-D MRI brain structure segmentation. In *Int. Conf. Med. Image Comput. Comput.-Assist. Interv., London, UK*, pages 575–583, Sept. 2009.

[127] L. Yang, B. Georgescu, Y. Zheng, P. Meer, and D. Comaniciu. 3D ultrasound tracking of the left ventricles using one-step forward prediction and data fusion of collaborative trackers. In *IEEE Comput. Soc. Conf. Comput. Vis. Pattern Recogn., Achorage, AK, USA*, June 2008.

[128] J. Zhang. The mean field theory in EM procedures for Markov random fields. *IEEE Trans. Signal Process.*, 40(10):2570–2583, Oct. 1992.

[129] Y. Zhang, M. Brady, and S. Smith. Segmentation of brain MR images through a hidden Markov random field model and the expectation-maximization algorithm. *IEEE Trans. Med. Imag.*, 20(1):45–57, Jan. 2001.

[130] Y. Zheng, A. Barbu, B. Georgescu, M. Scheuering, and D. Comaniciu. Fast automatic heart chamber segmentation from 3D CT data using marginal space learning and steerable features. In *IEEE Int. Conf. Comput. Vis., Rio de Janeiro, Brazil*, Oct. 2007.

[131] Y. Zheng, A. Barbu, B. Georgescu, M. Scheuering, and D. Comaniciu. Four-chamber heart modeling and automatic segmentation for 3D cardiac CT volumes using marginal space learning and steerable features. *IEEE Trans. Med. Imag.*, 27(11):1668–1681, Nov. 2008.

[132] J. M. Zook and K. M. Iftekharuddin. Statistical analysis of fractal-based brain tumor detection algorithms. *Magn. Reson. Imag.*, 23(5):671–678, June 2005.

Index